Larry Powell's

BIG BOOK
of Cake Decorating

Larry Powell's

Big Book
of Cake Decorating

By LARRY D. POWELL

Binford & Mort, Publishers

2536 S.E. Eleventh • Portland, Oregon 97202

Larry Powell's Big Book of Cake Decorating

Copyright under international
Pan-American copyright conventions
Copyright © 1977 by Larry D. Powell
No part of this book may be reproduced or
transmitted in any form or by any means
electronic or mechanical, including
photography, recording, or any information
storage and retrieval system, without
permission in writing from the publisher.
Library of Congress Catalog Card Number: 77-76026
ISBN: 0-8323-0286-4

Printed in the United States of America

First Edition 1977

To Deanna, Jillonne and Brock

Acknowledgments

I would like to express special appreciation to:

Margaret Lewis, my first art instructor.

Lilian Davis, for teaching me the skill and for helping me to find the inspiration to become a writer.

Harold and Josephine Bloodgood who encouraged me to become involved in the baking industry.

Shirley Ryan for the contribution of her "scarecrow" idea and for her help and encouragement over the years.

Guinn Hudon for assistance on the photography.

My hearty gratitude also to Jack and Lana Elmer and to Don and Marie Eklund for the use of their bakery facilities in preparing the photographs for this book.

Larry Powell
Author

Preface

"Whether it be for fun or profit, I hope you will consider LARRY POWELL'S BIG BOOK OF CAKE DECORATING. You will never regret it. It's the finest, most progressive cake-decorating book on the market. Never had I seen color combinations, flowers and composition created in such a realistic way. I was finally satisfied in all these areas because of a man named Larry Powell; truly a master decorator willing to share his talents with you and me."

Walter F. Cox
Finisher and Head Decorator
Baldwin, New York

"Larry Powell's book is a reflection of Larry himself. . .tremendous enthusiasm, fantastic imagination, and superb artistic talent. He is an inspiration to cake decorators around the world! . . .Here Larry shares his artistic talent and decorating skill for all of us to benefit from his unique knowledge. This creative book is a MUST for cake decorators everywhere!"

Barbara Boeving
Professional Cake Decorating
Instructor and Consultant
Concord, California

"Larry Powell is one of the most talented and innovative people in the baking industry today—a man who is destined to become a legend in the trade. Larry is dedicated to seeing beautiful and quality products come from the craft of the baker and has the skill and knowledge to communicate the methods. Anytime, anywhere, he is willing to help bakers with new ideas and new solutions to old problems. His skill, integrity and dedication stand out in the baking industry and have earned him respect and admiration throughout the country.

"Watching Larry Powell's new book materialize, over the years it has been in preparation, has been a fascinating and educational experience for me. There is always a new design, a new method, a new formula to be tried, to be reworked, to be perfected, to be presented to the baking industry to add more miracles to the art of cake decorating. Larry is the man who can make a dream-design, reality.

"It is my opinion that this book will very soon become the decorating bible of the baking industry. Nowhere else will bakers find the modern ideas and techniques so comprehensively and understandably presented. I am excited and eager to add this book to my library. I think other bakers will feel the same."

Jacob A. Elmer
Chef de Patisserie
Heidi's Swiss Pastries
Boring, Oregon

Contents

Introduction

Larry Powell's Big Book of Cake Decorating is a product of twenty-five years of study and research—first in the basic theory and the application of art, then in the practice and the development of new cake-decorating techniques.

Most of the introduction which follows was set on paper twelve years ago as I first realized that there was a real need for more complete information in many areas of cake decorating and that I might be able to utilize my art training to help to fill that void. To that point, most decorating classes, books, and demonstrations that I had encountered, left me with a deep desire to get more basic instructions, and with a feeling that there was a great lack of technical advice which obviously would be necessary to the achievement of the higher goals that I felt could be attained as a skilled craftsman in this fine art.

Please understand, I think some of these media of the past have made many worthwhile contributions to the decorating profession. I hold the conviction that all of these means of education, if well founded on basic principles, backed by original creativity, and proved by sound practical experience and application, do a reasonably good job of teaching. If they instill within the student a challenge to search further, and a desire to be original and creative in his work, it is not absolutely necessary that every phase of decorating be covered. In fact, it would be impossible to compile and to recount in any single edition all the facets of cake decorating known to those living, accomplished decorators, not to mention techniques already lost or not yet imagined.

It shall be my attempt in this "Big Book" to cover color and composition, materials, and equipment, mechanical techniques of pressure control, border work, flowers and figure piping, an introduction to cake sculpturing, and to provide a collection of illustrations and diagrams, as well as photographs of finished merchandise.

I anticipate that I shall likely review materials already covered by other authors on this subject. If, however, I am able to project fresh new insights for the student, with which he may develop his decorating skills, and thereby increase cake sales and cut labor time—or merely help him to find greater gratification in the art of cake decorating—I shall feel that this effort is immensely rewarding.

For countless times in the pages to come, I shall stress the great importance of practicing the basic motions and the control techniques which are essential to every form creatable from cake icing. No words can possibly express the tremendous necessity of constant practice and never-ending pursuit of perfection and reality. This desire and drive must come from within the student. I can only hope to plant the seed of enthusiasm, to provide the tools of knowledge and basic principles, and to share the ideas and creations born out of my own enthusiasm, as well as hours of study and unending practice. It is well to note that no man will ever exhaust the ideas and techniques possible in this or any other form of art, and each time a decorator stumbles onto an innovation, it will merely prove the point, and send him soaring into a whole new realm of ideas as a result of a single discovery.

Color and composition are, in my estimation, the least acknowledged, yet the most important components of cake decorating. In all of my observations of decorating classes, books and demonstrations, I have seldom encountered an instructor or author who emphasized the importance of these subjects.

I am positive that even the experienced professional decorator, who has never been exposed to the basic rules outlined in the second chapter, will benefit by markedly increasing the eye-appeal—the aesthetic quality of his work.

These basic rules are not designed to confine the decorator, but rather to give a basis for original creative exploration into a beautiful world of cake-decorating ART.

In the course on composition I shall try to cover the arrangement and layout of areas similar to the shapes of the cakes that the student will likely be decorating, as well as a simple lesson on perspective. If a decorator follows these basic practices in all his work, he will immediately increase the eye-appeal of the finished merchandise, and his customers will show a favorable reaction over a period of time by their buying response. No matter how neatly a student forms the decorations or how well he uses color combinations, without applying these basic rules of composition, his decorations will appear unexciting and lifeless even to the untrained eye.

Picture a skyscraper, under construction, as "the field of cake decorating," the FOUNDATION and FRAMEWORK representing COLOR and COMPOSITION. Obviously no contractor would attempt to construct an outer shell of this building without some form of undergirding support; so how can we expect a decorator to build a substantial, decorated-cake business without these basic rules?

I invite each student to pick up a decorating cone and join me step-by-step in one of the greatest, most gratifying fields of art.

Suggested Methods
For Study

This book is purposely arranged in the most logical order for learning and applying the components of cake decorating art.

READ THE COMPLETE TEXT

Before attempting any of the exercises in this book, read it once completely through. Make a note of the chapters that will require the greatest concentration and study. This first scan of the text will familiarize the reader with its total content so that he will appreciate the amount of time and effort it will require to study and to apply the information it contains.

The reader should be aware that time is a valuable resource and that it will be important to set aside adequate hours of uninterrupted time to study the less familiar information.

ASSEMBLE MATERIALS AND EQUIPMENT

After reading the first chapter on "Materials and Equipment," the reader should make every effort to acquire as many of the items as possible before attempting the following exercises that require icing and decorating tools. This will save valuable time needed for efficient, uninterrupted study. For the most part, icing will not be required for the study and practice of the first two chapters. In no way does this mean that these two chapters are of lesser importance to the knowledge one needs to become a fine decorating artist.

Powell

MAKE THE BASICS A HABIT

Color and composition are the BASICS for any art, and *their importance cannot be stressed too much!* Each student should practice these fundamental lessons until the skills become habit. These skills should be well developed before the decorator attempts to practice any of the exercises with icing. Knowledge of *color* and *composition* is so important that, without it, the possibility of a decorator producing a well-decorated cake, will be purely accidental.

PRACTICE CONTROL

Pressure control and *wrist action* are as important to the decorator as poise and balance are to a ballerina. Trying to decorate without good pressure control and wrist action could be likened to a hippopotamus doing a toe dance across lily pads on a lake. Practice of the exercises in Chapter III cannot be stressed enough. Not only is it important to learn the proper control and action, but the student should perfect these skills and then learn to perform them accurately with speed.

DEVELOP SPEED

Good decorators are not fine decorators until they can execute their skills with swiftness as well as accuracy. Speed is of prime importance to the professional decorator for the absolute necessity of adequate production. Speed also is important to the hobbyist decorator in the sense that it polishes skill. An icing-masterpiece doesn't necessarily mean hours of work, if the artist truly knows his skill. In fact, the speed and accuracy of such a masterpiece is a measure of the decorating artist's ability. The concept is reflected in cake decorations that are crisp, with flowing lines, but uncluttered. It is absolutely unnecessary for every open area on the cake to be decorated. Many professionals, as well as amateurs, seem to feel that it is a *must* to fill the total surface of a cake before they can say it is decorated; this is a trap that should be avoided, as it often results in less eye-pleasing compositions and in cluttered designs.

THE CHALLENGE OF ROSES

The chapter on flowers begins with the most basic blossom, the rose. This blossom provides an extension of the training on pressure control and wrist action. It adds the skill of manipulating a wooden skewer and requires that the decorator combine what he has previously learned with the task of coordination.

Repeated practice of forming the rose blossom is a *must* before the reader proceeds to the studies of the other flowers in this text. Even for experienced decorators, this new concept of creating a rose will be a challenge; perhaps an even greater challenge than for the beginner, for it will require a change in older, previously developed habits that are very difficult to break. Every other blossom in the book is based on the structure of this rose. The student's success with them will be extremely dependent on the thorough knowledge and training that results from practicing this instructor's style of rose.

THE ARTIST IN YOU

Certainly, a previous background in art training would be a valuable asset to any decorating student. Many students who possess a natural creative talent for drawing will have already acquired such training. Even the person who has a "natural" ability in art must also have guidance and training. No one artist in history could claim inborn knowledge of all the theories and fundamentals of color, composition, and anatomy. Many have made their contributions to the development of art, just as this author hopes he has made contributions to the expansion of cake-decorating art. It is important to remember that each artist's abilities are a composite result of the efforts of those artists before him. He is merely another link in a long chain of contributors. Many students of this author's seminars have been amazed at their own hidden natural gift of ability. Practice on the fundamental theories and rules of drawing the human figure, that are expressed in Chapter V of this text, may reveal hidden talent in many readers who didn't know the ability existed within them. If this special talent is evident upon the student's first attempts at drawing with the aid of the guidelines herein, he needs only to cultivate it with practice and application. Further research, outside this text, may be desired and is available at libraries and book stores; but the foundation is here and should be adequate if it is backed up with patience, study and effort.

RESOURCE FILE

It will be almost a necessity for the professional decorator who develops his talent of figure piping to acquire a mass of resource pictures for his work.

No one person has the background to be aware of the vast variety of sports, hobbies and occupations, and of the implements and equipment that are associated with each. Magazines, telephone books, newspapers, and catalogs provide excellent pictures. Many pictures even reveal the peculiarities of stance or motion that identify a particular sport or type of work, and the equipment that is associated with it.

A notebook or filing cabinet that is divided into categories of sports, hobbies, occupations, animals, and types of transportation would be a good start. Consider other materials such as special occasions, holiday items, religious materials, and military and fraternal organization insignias, too.

For the serious artist who plans to pursue special portraits, etc., it would be advisable to include a file on faces, hairstyles, and costumes.

CHAPTER I
Materials and Equipment

Icing Formulas
Special Materials
Proper Equipment
How to Ice Cakes

Materials and Equipment

Each student should become familiar with the tools and materials of the decorator's trade and with how to use them properly. This chapter provides a list of the equipment necessary to complete the exercises in this book. The list is accompanied by a detailed description, item-by-item. After the reader studies this chapter he should avail himself of these items before he attempts the subsequent exercises.

Following is a list of some of the necessary equipment and materials of real importance to the fulfillment of the studies in this book:

Formula for buttercream icing used for decorating
Food color
Parchment paper decorating cones
Decorating tips
All purpose edging tip
Paint brushes
Palette knife
Scissors
Bowl knives (icing spatulas)
Plastic drinking straws
Ice cream cones
Firm non-corrugated cardboard
Hot plate
Measuring can or water pot
Practice board with plastic top
Bowls
Turntable
Airbrush (see Chapter II, page 46)

BUTTERCREAM FOR PRACTICE AND HOME USE

1 pound powdered (confectioner's) sugar
1/4 cup evaporated milk
1 cup shortening (white)
1 teaspoon vanilla
1/2 teaspoon salt

Blend the powdered sugar, salt, vanilla, and milk to a smooth, stiff paste. Add the shortening and mix until all the ingredients are thoroughly incorporated.

DECORATING BUTTERCREAM FOR PROFESSIONAL USE

50 pounds powdered (confectioner's) sugar   3 ounces salt
 6 pounds cold water   3 ounces vanilla
25 pounds emulsified cake shortening

Blend the powdered sugar, water, salt, and vanilla to a smooth paste. This will be very stiff and should be mixed at low speed, only long enough to saturate and to remove all the lumps from the sugar.

Add the shortening in one- or two-pound portions and mix at medium speed until completely incorporated. Caution: scrape down the sides of the mixing bowl thoroughly in this stage; do not overmix. Overmixing the buttercream will cause excessive aeration that will be particularly detrimental to smooth figure work.

TROUBLE SHOOTING FOR PROBLEMS WITH BUTTERCREAM

Occasionally problems may develop with this buttercream. Many of the difficulties can be traced to the ingredients or to the mixing procedure.

This buttercream works best if it is mixed at least a day before it is to be used. After it sits it will become aerated, but most of the bubbles should disappear when it is remixed. Caution should be employed here; the remixing should be done by hand or on the lowest speed with a machine. It is best to remix only the amount needed for short periods of time. Portions for colored icings will have adequate remixing in the process of blending in the paste colors. These colored mixtures should be remixed occasionally to assure consistent smoothness.

Overmixing or mixing at excessive speed will cause the icing to be severely-aerated—once this has occurred, there is no remedy. If the icing is simply too soft, the problem could be caused by the shortening. If the shortening is stored in too warm a place, it will not produce firm buttercream. Since this is a real problem in the summertime, particularly in the warmer climates, one should chill the water before it is added in the first stage. Sometimes the fault is a result of poor quality shortening, so it would therefore be advisable for the decorator to experiment with different brands.

If the icing is lumpy, the problem could be from sugar that has been exposed to moisture. Also, lumps may be prevalent if, in the second stage of the mixing procedure, the bowl has not been adequately scraped clean. The bowl should be scraped all the way to the bottom at least two times.

If, in the process of decorating, the buttercream seems too tacky or too elastic it may be due to the sugar. Only powdered cane sugar will produce the best quality buttercream for decorating.

DETAILED LIST OF MATERIALS AND EQUIPMENT

FOOD COLOR

Food colors, for most practical purposes, are available in paste and liquid form. If food colors are available from more than one source, it may pay to shop around and to test different brands. Some are dull and make it difficult to mix truly clear icing colors, particularly if a decorator wishes to purchase only primary colors and to mix his own secondary tones. Some pinks and reds tend to have a slight bluish cast, rather than being bright and pure. Some yellows are golden, whereas a lemon yellow produces truer secondary colors. Since sky blue will have a greenish cast, try to find a good royal blue. Some blues will be rather muddy and dull. Of all colors, red paste color is probably the most difficult to find in a suitable hue. A flame red is good, and can sometimes be achieved by mixing a Christmas red and an equal amount of brilliant pink and a small portion of lemon yellow. Too much yellow will result in an overpowering orange appearance.

Red, pink, yellow, blue, and black will be a sufficient selection to create most any of the colors. If the use of much brown is anticipated, it might be well to add brown coloring to the list. Otherwise, mix the brown needed from a combination of orange and green.

Due to the high fat content of buttercream, *paste food colors* work best for coloring the icing.

Liquid colors tend to soften and to break down the buttercream, making it difficult to form good blossoms and firm figures, and will be of little use unless an airbrush is available (see Chapter II, APPLICATION OF BACKGROUNDS).

To get the most out of paste food colors, it will be helpful to follow a few simple mixing directions. First dip some paste from the food coloring jar with a bowl knife. If the paste seems a little dry or stiff, smooth it out against the side of the bowl or on a hard, smooth surface, with just a little buttercream. Little by little, add more buttercream until the desired tone is achieved. Blending the colors in this fashion will prevent concentration of little lumps of unblended coloring paste from clogging the decorating tip.

PARCHMENT PAPER
DECORATING CONES

For the cone, place a triangular sheet of parchment paper on the workbench. One of the three sides of the triangle will be longer than the other two; call this side X. The point of the triangle opposite side X is P. Placing the triangle so that Point P is aimed toward the nearest edge of the workbench, consider the left point of the paper as Flap L and the right point as Flap R.

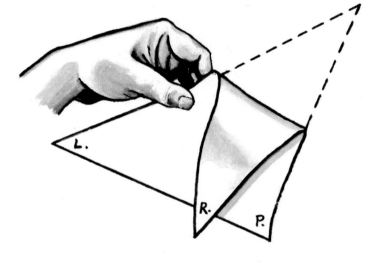

Grip Side X *midway* with the tips of the thumb and forefinger of the left hand; hold the paper triangle so that Point P is aimed downward. Lap the paper so that Flap R rests over Flap L.

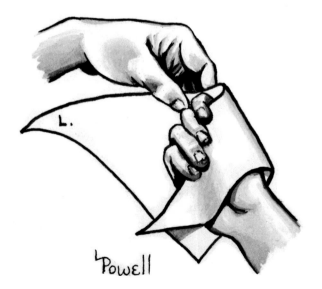

Slip the right hand, palm upward, between the layers of paper and get a firm grip on the X edge of Flap R about three or four inches from the left thumb-hold.

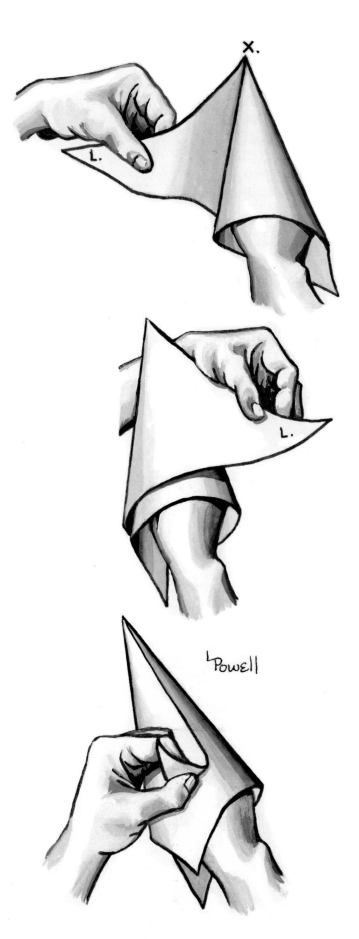

Do not allow the right hand to slip from the edge of the paper when beginning to twist the R half counterclockwise, forming a point at the position of the left thumb. As the cone takes form, gently slide the left hand toward the point of Flap L.

Interchange the positions of the left thumb and forefinger and, without dropping the end of the paper, wrap Flap L around the cone in the right hand.

At this time, the right hand should be positioned palm-up, and the seam where Flap L meets the cone should lie on the upper side. If the tip of the cone does not form a tightly closed point, pull the point of Flap L firmly toward the right elbow, maintaining a firm grip inside the cone. Slip the left hand around the outside of the cone, turning counter-clockwise with the right hand so that the tip remains tight. Now slide the left hand down to flatten the point of the cone to secure it and to prevent it from unwrapping before removing the right hand from inside.

25

Snip or tear enough from the point of the cone to accommodate a decorating tip; insert the tip and fill the cone with icing. Hold it securely with the left hand by gripping the cone just at the top edge of the decorating tip to prevent it from unwinding as the icing is placed inside.

DECORATING TIPS

No. 104 rose
No. 125 rose
No. 16 star
No. 18 star

Two No. 104 rose tips and six or eight No. 125 rose tips will be adequate to take care of most floral decorating needs. Of course it's entirely possible to get by with fewer, but this selection allows the decorator freedom to have cones of several colors made up at one time for cakes with different themes.

One of each of the star tips will be sufficient for practice or for cake bordering. On certain occasions it might be good to have a No. 14 star tip for finer border work.

ALL PURPOSE EDGING TIP

The all purpose edging tip is made from a No. 180 rose tip. This, like the ordinary rose tip, has a wedge-opening that must be reshaped so that it is the same width from top to bottom. Use a knife or screwdriver to spread the narrow point. Next, with needle-nosed pliers, slightly mash the wide end of the opening so that its width is about 1/16 to 3/32 of an inch. Square the point of the opening by squeezing it firmly with the pliers, then carefully flatten the wavy side-walls of the opening. When completed, the opening of the tip should be one long slot, even in width from the top to the bottom.

Because of its great size, this tip must be used in a fabric pastry bag, rather than in a parchment decorating cone. This handy tool will be most useful in applying icing to the sides of sheet cakes. It will require some practice before the decorator learns to control an adequate amount of pressure to do the job, but for those who are patient enough to learn, the benefits of this tool will be extremely rewarding.

This tip will also be helpful for those students who wish to try their hand at cake sculpturing. Each decorator will undoubtedly find many other applications for this marvelous edging tip.

PAINT BRUSHES

No. 0
No. 6
Half-inch
One-inch

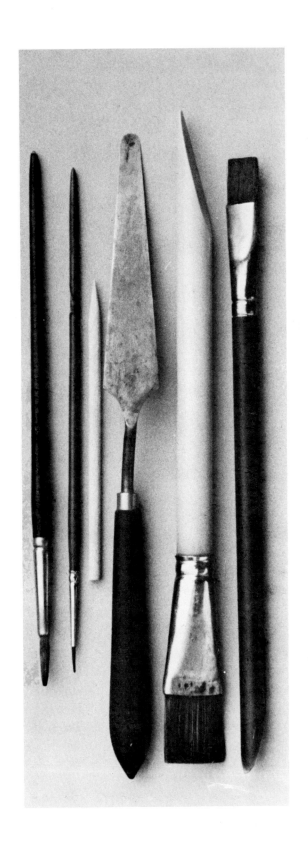

Find good quality artist's tools. Select soft camel or sable water color brushes. Usually a Number 0 and a Number 6 will be acceptable, although the sizes differ according to different manufacturers, so it may be trial and error selection at first. It is not imperative that a decorator have a one-inch brush unless he wishes to do a lot of portrait or sculpture work. The half-inch brush will be fine for practice and for most of the required smoothing of piped figures.

Be sure that the brushes are cleaned with warm water after each day's use, and see to it that they are carefully stored with the bristles "up" to prevent their misshaping and damage. Quality brushes, with good care, should last several years with daily use.

PALETTE KNIFE

Buy a quality palette knife. Test different brands and select a nice limber blade for the best job. Palette knives come either with straight or with offset handles. The offset handle style allows more freedom of movement. The blade should be about four inches long, and tapered to a narrow, rounded tip.

WOODEN MEAT SKEWERS

The standard meat skewers run about five to six inches in length, and are sharpened to a point at one end. If these skewers are not available through a regular decorating supply house, check with a local butcher.

SCISSORS

Choose sharp scissors of a comfortable length to work with. Tastes tend to differ from one individual to another. Just make sure that the blades are thin and finely pointed.

BOWL KNIVES (ICING SPATULAS)

These are items to be selected according to individual taste. They are available in different widths and lengths, as well as in flexible or stiff varieties. Each knife has its particular advantage depending on its use. It is wise, but not mandatory, to have several on hand for use in different colored icings.

PLASTIC DRINKING STRAWS

Plastic straws are available in thin bar straws, or larger diameter milkshake-type. Both have their applications in the cake decorating art, so have a supply of each on hand. The thinner straws will be used for figure piping; the larger for flowers.

ICE CREAM CONES

Have a full carton of cones on hand for the construction of mini-sculptures. Be sure that they are the old-fashioned pointed cones, not the flat-bottomed cup-type.

CARDBOARD

Firm cardboard, not corrugated, about the thickness of cake box material is best. It should have a white finish on both sides. It needn't be more than about four inches by eight inches for most decorating purposes, and will probably be cut into smaller pieces depending on its use. Keep in mind that the stock must be fairly sturdy, but capable of being cut with ordinary scissors when folded double. This is the best gauge for selecting the proper weight cardboard.

Corrugated cardboard, aside from its familiar use for sheet cake boards and for layer cake circles, will be required as the base boards for the ice cream cone sculptures in the final chapter of this text.

HOT PLATE

Any hot plate with controlled heating is fine. This writer prefers the solid burner rather than the type with coiled wire elements. The solid element has an easier surface to clean, and probably will last longer for use with the sugary icings.

WATER POT

A sauce pan will work fine, but a one- or two-quart stainless steel measure is perfect for heating the water used for dipping the paint brushes to smooth the figure piping. Pans with long handles may be unhandy to work with, and can cause accidental spills and burns. As a convenient alternative, an electric coffee percolator works pretty well, although most models do not keep the water temperature as near boiling as is preferable.

PRACTICE BOARD

A good practice board can be made with a piece of plywood with a hard, non-staining plastic top. This provides an excellent work surface with minimum clean-up problems. If such a board is not conveniently available, use waxed paper or work directly on a bench or table top.

BOWLS

Since this decorating buttercream tends to develop a slight crust on its surface, it is handy to have plastic bowls with the type of lids that seal. This is particularly advisable if the icings are to be stored for several days.

Provide one bowl for each of the frequently used colors, as well as some empties in case it becomes necessary to mix special colors for a particular project. The best set-up would be one bowl each for: black, brown, flesh, red, bright pink, soft pink, lavender or purple, deep blue, soft blue, deep green, yellow green, bright yellow, soft yellow, and orange. Second choice would be one each for black, brown, red, pink, lavender, blue, green, yellow, and orange.

TURNTABLE

Standard cake decorating turntables are available through regular bakery supply houses. Plastic kitchen storage turntables are available in most department stores and are suitable substitutes.

This completes the list of most items that will be necessary for cake decorating. The only items on this list that will need periodic replacement are the food colorings and parchment papers. The rest require only an original investment and will last for years. Trying to work without proper equipment and materials is like attempting to decorate with one's hands tied behind his back, so assemble the proper tools before attempting the exercises in this text.

PREPARING THE CAKE FOR ICING

In order to produce a good looking decorated cake, the preparation and icing process is very important. Refrigerate or freeze the cake until it is well chilled before attempting to slice layers for filling or to carve pieces of cake for sculpturing. This will allow greater ease of handling and will lessen breakage and crumbling problems.

By slicing each layer to transform a two layer cake into four thinner layers, the cake will accommodate two additional portions of filling. This extra filling adds greater flavor and improves the keeping quality of the cake.

ICING THE PREPARED CAKE

After the cake is properly chilled and the layers are assembled, the reader may find that the following suggestions will make icing the top and sides an easy task.

HELPFUL HINTS FOR ICING THE CAKE

1. Use plenty of icing (excessive icing can be scraped off to a desired thickness).

2. Icing should be of good spreading consistency (if too firm it will tear the cake; if too soft, it may run and cause the borders to droop).

3. Apply the icing to the top of the cake, then to the sides, and smooth the top last.

PROPER USE OF THE BOWL KNIFE

The bowl knife is an important instrument to be used firmly yet gently as a pusher, not a smasher. It is, therefore, most important that it be held properly so that it can be easily manipulated and guided with smoothness and accuracy.

Grip the edges of the bowl knife blade, where it enters the handle, between the pads of the thumb and forefinger. Allow the handle to be cradled in the remaining three fingers. This grip allows the bowl knife to be rolled between the thumb and forefinger so that both edges of the blade can be used alternately—the first edge to smooth as the knife is guided to the left; the second, turned down to smooth the icing as it is guided back to the right.

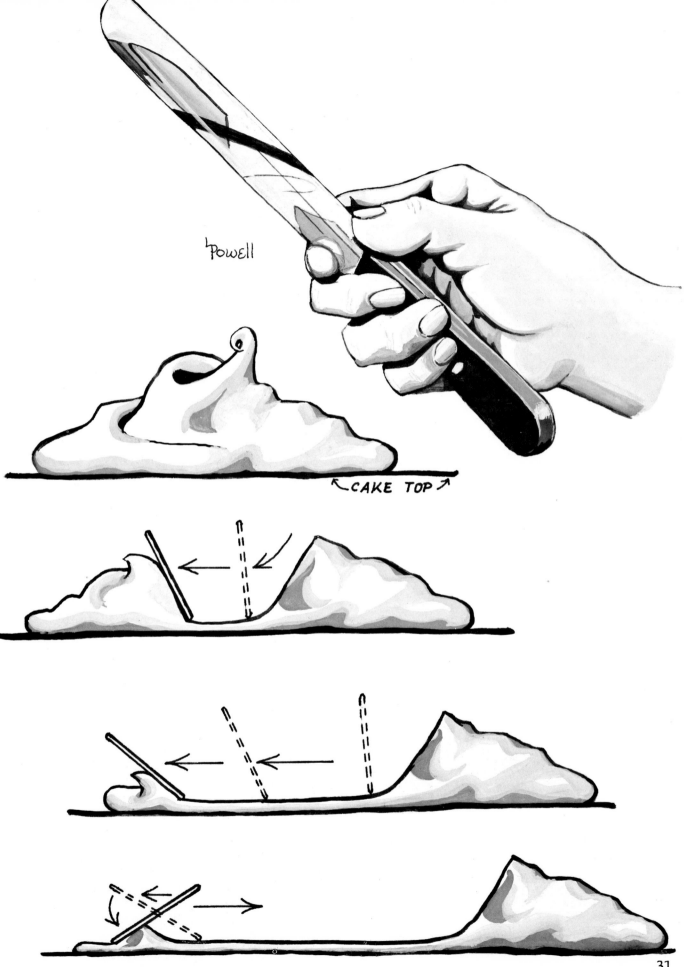

CAKE TOP

Place the cake on a turntable. Using either the bowl knife or a mixing spoon, drop a large dollop of icing onto the cake. This amount will, of course, vary and should be estimated in accordance with the area of the cake top.

Use the bowl knife to spread the icing toward the outer edge of the cake top, making certain to cover the top completely to the outer rim. Don't be concerned if a little icing extends beyond the edge. Gently scrape the excess icing to the desired thickness, taking care not to reveal any of the cake's surface.

Turn the cake while holding the bowl knife in a nearly vertical position against the top rim to remove the excess icing at the edge. Before proceeding to the next step, scrape or wipe the bowl knife clean to avoid depositing crumbs into the icing bowl.

Apply a generous amount of icing to a small segment of the side of the cake. Be certain that the bowl knife blade is sufficiently covered so that the icing extends to the full height of the side of the cake, from bottom to top. Repeat this process around the circumference of the cake until its sides are completely and generously covered.

Clean the knife and gently press the edge of the blade against the side of the cake. Continually turn the cake several revolutions to smooth the sides. Some of the excess icing will be forced upward to the top rim of the cake.

Remove the excess icing with a scraping motion, moving from the outer rim toward the center of the cake. Finish the top to a level smoothness with the fewest strokes possible. Round layers may be smoothed with the cake in a spinning motion. A sheet cake is best smoothed by sweeping motions across its full length.

ADDITIONAL MATERIALS AND EQUIPMENT

There are numerous tools, icings, and materials which are not necessary to the fulfillment of the studies in this book but that may be of interest to the readers. The following list is provided to acquaint the student with a few of these items and with their applications.

CLOTH PASTRY BAG

Cloth pastry bags are preformed decorating cones and can be used in place of parchment paper. They are available in various sizes and are particularly convenient for border work as they can be easily refilled when necessary. This author does not recommend the use of pastry bags for practice purposes, but strongly advocates their use for experienced decorators.

DECORATING TIPS

Decorating tips of almost any size or shape imaginable are available through various markets. Although only the few mentioned earlier in this chapter are recommended for the studies in this book, the readers should be allowed and encouraged to experiment with any tips that they should desire. These include tips for leaves, string work, unusual borders, lily of the valley, and drop flowers (violets, forget-me-nots, and other tiny blossoms).

NYLON PLASTIC COUPLINGS

These couplings are adapters designed for use in pastry bags to provide the convenience of changing from one decorating tip to another without emptying the icing from the bag.

ROYAL ICING

Royal icing sets up hard and is primarily used for elaborate, make-up-ahead-of-time lattice and scrolls for decorating Victorian style wedding cakes. Its present day commercial use has been relegated to usually less ornate display cakes for retail bakeries. However, many hobbyists have time to pursue this pleasurable form of decorating.

> 3 pounds powdered (confectioner's) sugar
> 8 (1 cup) egg whites *or* 1/3 cup meringue powder
>   plus 1 cup water
> 1 teaspoon cream of tartar

Blend the sugar, cream of tartar, and just enough egg white in a mixer to make a smooth paste. Add the remainder of the egg whites and mix until the icing forms stiff peaks.

This icing should always be covered with a damp cloth during use, then stored in air-tight containers. Decorations from this icing should be made on waxed paper and must be allowed to sit untouched for twenty-four hours.

CHAPTER II
Basic Rules of Color and Composition

Mixing Colors
Color Wheel
Background Color
Three-Dimensional Landscapes
Airbrush
Basic Composition
Perspective

Basic Rules of Color and Composition

There are three basic colors or hues: RED, BLUE, and YELLOW. These three extractions from the spectrum are referred to as primary colors; "primary" because, when mixed in various amounts and combinations, these colors can be blended to create every color visible to man. The terms color and hue are synonymous.

It will be necessary for the student to give close attention to the following color wheels and to practice mixing and applying the colors as illustrated. For valuable experience and for easier understanding, EVERY STUDENT SHOULD MAKE HIS OWN COLOR WHEEL on a large piece of white cardboard or paper. He should select a piece of cardboard that will accommodate at least an eight-inch circle to allow adequate space for the placement of colors.

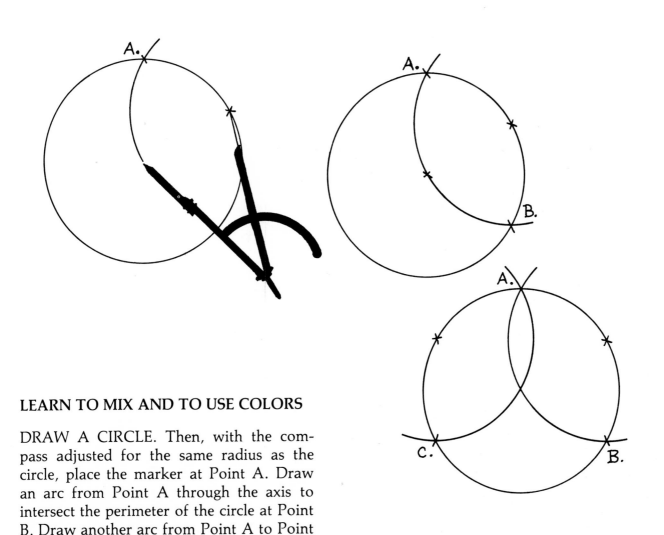

LEARN TO MIX AND TO USE COLORS

DRAW A CIRCLE. Then, with the compass adjusted for the same radius as the circle, place the marker at Point A. Draw an arc from Point A through the axis to intersect the perimeter of the circle at Point B. Draw another arc from Point A to Point C. Points A, B, and C indicate the positions for the primary colors.

PRIMARY COLORS

Beginning at the mark at the top of the circle, apply a spot of bright yellow icing. Proceeding clockwise to the second mark, add a smear of blue, following with vivid red at the remaining position. These represent the primary colors.

Just outside the color wheel, next to the red, place a spot of brilliant pink. Most red paste colors available do not represent a true red, adequate for blending with other colors. The result is usually muddy or drab tones. A good true pink will, on the other hand, provide bright, almost fluorescent tones. This is the reason for using pink paste color instead of red to mix other colors on the color wheel.

SECONDARY COLORS

Mark the circle exactly midway between each of the primary colors. The hues at these points will represent the secondary color scheme, and their identities can be revealed by mixing equal intensities of the two primary colors on either side of their positions on the color wheel. Hence, from yellow and blue comes green. Mixing blue and red produces violet, and red and yellow combine to create orange.

Looking at the color wheel, one is aware that yellow is the color nearest *white* (a term to signify the absence of color). Opposite yellow on the color wheel is violet, the most intense color visible to man.

INTENSITY

At this point it is necessary to explain what is meant by the *intensity of colors*. Some colors have greater strength than others. For instance, the pigments in red and blue have more power than yellow, and this strength is the quality of intensity which one should be aware of in different colors. Therefore, when red is mixed with orange, yellow, or green, it will require a smaller portion of red coloring than the other color in the mixture to produce the ultimately desired hue.

40

Colors produced from blending equal intensities of a primary color and its secondary companion at either side are yellow-green, blue-green, blue-violet, red-violet, red-orange, and yellow-orange. These fractions of color can be likened to the indications of time on a clock. That is, the spectrum has no separation from one color to the other, just as time has no separation from one second to the next. Therefore, these fractions of color are merely tools to define and to identify what one's eyes perceive. It is possible to mix literally millions of color variations by this method alone, without even taking into consideration color tints or shades.

COMPLEMENTARY COLORS

If a double-ended arrow were placed on an axis at the center of the color wheel, the colors at either end of that arrow would represent the complementary colors.

If a color is mixed with its complement directly across the color wheel, it will render a form of grey. Greying a color can be achieved by adding to it a bit of its complement. Add a drop of orange to its complement to *grey* blue. The more orange added to this mixture, the greyer the blue becomes, until it reaches saturation—this will be the truest grey possible from this blend. This saturation would take place at the exact center of the color wheel; beyond this point, instead of greying the blue with the orange, the orange would be greyed with the blue.

The process of greying colors will be most helpful when one must match the color of the buttercream to a particular swatch of material. Often a bride-to-be will submit colored ribbon, or a piece of material like that which she plans to incorporate into her wedding. Very frequently these colors are not pure blends of primary colors, and the decorator will have to experiment with color combinations and may not always be successful. The chances of finding the correct mixture are greater, once the decorator has had experience with greying colors.

TINTS

Tints are produced when any hue is made lighter. With decorating buttercream, this will take place when white and colored icings are combined. Mixing soft tints from intense hues such as red, blue or dark green requires a comparatively greater quantity of white. It, therefore, would be better to add a bit of colored icing to white and to work toward a preferred tint rather than to attempt to lighten the color by adding white. The technique for making color tints will be particularly helpful to the student when he prepares the edges of flower petals. See the suggestions and the background color chart on pages 44 and 45. Also see THE PARCHMENT CONE, FILLING AND BLENDING on page 128.

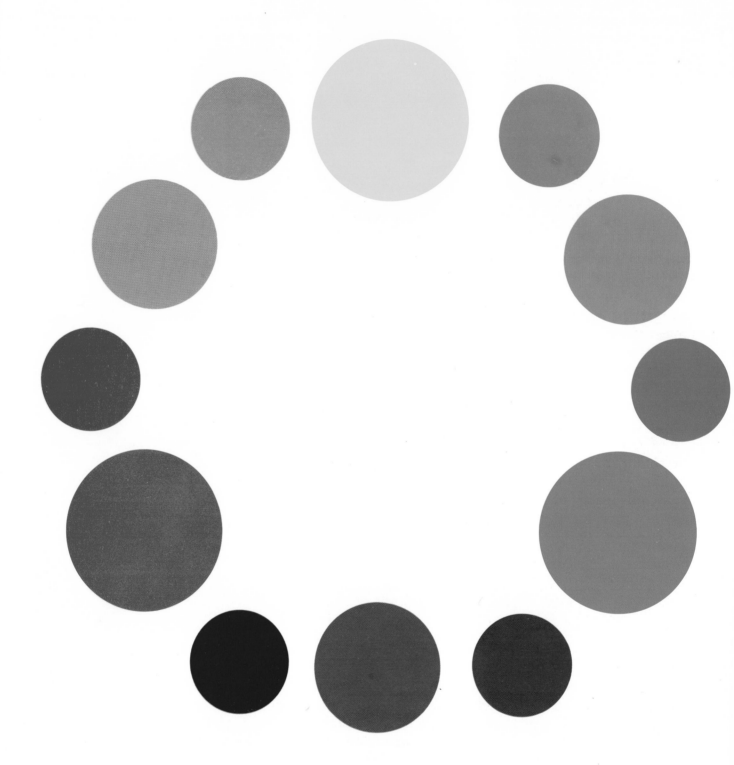

SHADES

Shades are the opposite of tints. They are hues with the addition of black to darken them. As white is the absence of color, black is the combination of all colors in the spectrum. If it is not available, black can be made by mixing red, blue and yellow paste colors into a very small amount of icing, but it takes a great quantity of each of these primary colors to make a black icing anywhere nearly equal in intensity to that which can be produced from the pre-blended black food coloring which comes from the manufacturers.

THEME AND BACKGROUND COLORS

The object of background color or composition on a cake is to enhance the theme of the decoration. The background should never detract from the main subject, either by clashing with the colors, or by cluttering the scene. If the subject of the decoration is a floral design, the decorator should decide what color(s) the flowers should be, or should abide by the customer's preference if the cake is a special order, then select a background color to integrate the whole design and to produce the appearance of a well planned work of art.

Some decorators, even after studying colors and mixing different hues to create a color wheel, still have difficulty in selecting the proper go-together color schemes. People seem either to have a natural feel for color combinations, or they have to train their visual senses with hard work and practice.

For the decorators who find color perception difficult to master, the chart on the following page may prove to be an invaluable guide. These combinations are always acceptable. The three columns represent suitable color selections for the floral arrangement, plus a choice of harmonious background hues. Each of the first two columns lists two variegated combinations of colors for the flowers. The first hue in each column represents the main color of the flower, and the second hue is to be used for the soft tone at the tip of the petal. For example, in the first line on the chart, some of the flowers on the cake will be pale yellow with white tips. The other flowers on the cake will be bright yellow with pale yellow tips. Then either yellow, green, or violet can be selected for the background color.

Most floral arrangements, even when the blossoms are variegated, are more eye pleasing if they are designed with flowers of two distinct hues. Therefore, a cake's decoration will be more interesting if the decorator uses a combination such as red and pink roses. In this case, he could place red roses randomly on the stem arrangement, and then fill out the bouquet with pink roses instead of having the whole floral design of just one hue.

44

COMBINATIONS OF COLORS FOR FLOWERS AND BACKGROUNDS

The three columns on this chart show color combinations for flowers and a choice of suitable background hues. The first column lists the variegated tones for part of the blossoms, the second lists variegated tones for flowers that will be compatible with the first blossoms in the arrangement, and the third column shows color hues which will provide a complementary background for the floral design.

Main Petal Color	Tip Toner	Main Petal Color	Tip Toner	Choice of Background (Select one)
pale yellow	WHITE	BRIGHT YELLOW	pale yellow	yellow, green, violet
pale orange	pale yellow	BRIGHT ORANGE	pale orange	yellow, orange, green
pale orange	WHITE	pale orange	pale pink	orange, pink, green
RED	(none)	WHITE	(none)	pink, green, white
RED	BRIGHT PINK	BRIGHT PINK	pale pink	pink, green, white
pale pink	WHITE	BRIGHT PINK	pale pink	pink, green, violet
pale violet	pale pink	pale violet	WHITE	pink, violet, blue
pale violet	WHITE	BRIGHT VIOLET	pale violet	violet, pink, blue
pale violet	pale blue	pale blue	WHITE	violet, blue, yellow

Brown or gold backgrounds are good alternative choices for cakes which are decorated with yellow or orange tones. Floral arrangements in these colors also are attractive when they are set over blends of brown and green.

Tan or bronze-toned petals, tipped with white, golden yellow, or light orange, can be used to accompany flowers of yellow and orange tones. These are particularly appropriate combinations for flowers like chrysanthemums, dahlias, and daisies, since brown and bronze hues are common to these species. Colors in this range are excellent choices for men's cakes but are favored by many women, too.

APPLICATION OF BACKGROUND COLOR AND TEXTURE

Backgrounds can be handled two ways: the decorator can cover the top of the cake with colored icing, or he can spray the iced cake with an airbrush. Colored icing backgrounds which are applied to the cake with a bowl knife are almost necessarily limited to a solid tone over the whole top of the cake. Airbrushed backgrounds, on the other hand, may be applied with such complete control that a cake top can be sprayed with a light mist, and then can be oversprayed around the outer edge with a darker tone or with even another hue. For production speed, the airbrush is unequaled and should be strongly considered as a necessary tool to be included in the decorating equipment for all professionals. Many amateurs also are discovering that the airbrush is a worthwhile investment, especially if they do a lot of decorating and want to create unusual settings for their scenic and floral designs.

The airbrush allows a decorator to spray colored backgrounds on his cakes in a fraction of the time that it would take for him to apply colored icing to the cake tops with a bowl knife. It offers him greater capabilities of design, and is almost a necessity if the decorator wishes to attempt the versatile stenciled backgrounds like those on many of the cakes illustrated in this book. Stenciled backgrounds add a special illusion of depth to most figure-piped designs and they heighten the observer's interest in an otherwise ordinary floral composition.

AIRBRUSH

When shopping for an airbrush, the decorator should select one which can be manipulated to produce either a fine line or a wide fog with one easy-to-operate control button. Avoid one that requires readjustment of separate knobs and buttons for each different function. Air supply devices vary from small pumps (like those used for aquariums) to larger compressors which come in a practically limitless number of sizes. Some small pumps produce a minimum of air pressure—these work well for spraying close to the icing. Regular compressors, however, do seem to produce a finer mist, and any of them can be easily equipped with a pressure reducer valve so that they work equally well for close-up work.

There exist basically two types of airbrushes: one that syphons the liquid from bottles, and another which is equipped with a reservoir into which liquid colors are fed, a drop or two at a time. Airbrushes should be handled with reasonable care so as not to damage their finely machined parts, and they should be disassembled occasionally and washed in warm water and detergent.

LEARN TO USE THE AIRBRUSH

The airbrush is a finely tuned instrument, but it takes only a little practice to learn to use it with expertise. One should use only ordinary liquid food color in an airbrush, and, for best results, the color should not be diluted. The decorator should learn to control his particular airbrush so that it will produce as fine a mist as he desires without his resorting to thinning the color. DO NOT USE "liquid paste" food colors, not even if they are diluted with distilled water; they have a tendency to clog the airbrush and will cause the spray to be emitted in spatters rather than in a fine mist.

It would be a good idea for the decorator to practice spraying on white paper rather than on an iced cake when he first is learning to use an airbrush. The student should experiment with various effects to learn the precise capabilities of his particular instrument. To produce a fine line, the tip of the airbrush must be held very close to the surface of the icing or practice paper, and the control button should be only slightly depressed or pulled back—the direction of control depends on the make of airbrush. For a wide mist, when a more overall fog is desirable, the airbrush should be held quite a distance back from the surface of the cake, and the button should be pulled nearly all the way back (or for some models, depressed most of the way). There are, of course, many variations in between and that is why it is important for a beginner to practice on something other than an iced cake, so that he will really get the feel of the airbrush and will know exactly what kind of performance to expect from it.

When the use of airbrushes was first adapted to cake decorating, their primary function was to apply overall color to the top of the iced cake. One of the nice effects that can be achieved is the lightly misted color over the whole cake top that is then darkened around the outer perimeter to produce a shadowed frame around the decoration. This technique should be practiced on paper after the student is familiar with how his airbrush operates; then, he should experiment with a second color for the darker frame of mist.

With the evolution of cake decorating came the use of the overhead image projector, and the airbrush played a significant role. All manner of cartoons and insignia could be copied on cakes—first drawn with black piping jell or black buttercream, then colored with an airbrush.

Now stencils are widely used to produce an endless array of designs and scenic backgrounds, allowing the decorator even more creative latitude.

There are almost no limitations for the resourceful, imaginative, creative cake decorator. The airbrush offers the buttercream artist boundless ways to explore and to expand his decorating skills.

STENCILED BACKGROUNDS

Stencils are available under the name MAGIC-MIST™ and are specially designed and are constructed of washable plastic for airbrushing backgrounds on cakes. If the decorator should prefer to make his own, stencils can be cut from lightweight cardboard or from "Bristol paper." Stencil knives, available at most art supply houses, work best; however, sharp scissors can be used for cutting some stencils if the paper is not too heavy and if the design is not extremely intricate. Stenciling can be done atop any kind of buttercream. Softer French-type buttercream-iced cakes either must be chilled until the icing's surface is firm to the touch, or they must be protected with a "nylon net" cover screen before the stencil is placed on them. Nylon net can be purchased at most fabric shops, and is available in an assortment of "mesh" sizes. One should choose the finest mesh that he can buy, for best results. The net should be stretched across a frame cut from a half-sheet cake board. Cut the corrugated board so that its outer edges form a frame about three-quarters of an inch wide, and fasten the nylon net onto the frame with masking tape. The resulting screen can be layed directly on top of a cake that is iced with soft buttercream so that the stencils will not rest directly in contact with the icing. Then the stencil and the screen can be lifted without marring the iced cake.

This portion of the text is provided merely as a means to acquaint the student with the basics of stenciling on cakes. This author has written a book entitled "CAKE DECORATING WITH MAGIC-MIST™ STENCILS AND YOUR AIRBRUSH," which is available with sets of stencils or can be purchased separately at most of the suppliers where "THE BIG BOOK OF CAKE DECORATING" is sold; it offers tips and ideas for using the airbrush and stencils, and explains, in detail, how to create unlimited designs and special effects with them.

USE A NYLON NET SCREEN

Advice on how to choose the right nylon net and on the technique for making the cardboard screen are outlined earlier on the page. Cakes that are iced with a type of buttercream which dries with a slight crust do not require the use of the screen under the stencils.

Place the screen on top of the cake, but make certain that the cake is iced as smoothly as it possibly can be.

This framed nylon screen is available in MAGIC-MIST™ Set No. 2.

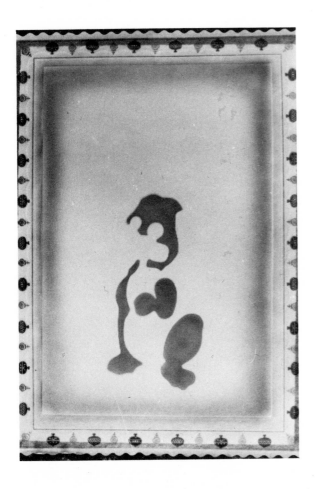

SPRAY THE PATTERN

Gently rest the stencil on top of the cake (or on the screen). Do not scoot the stencil if it is necessary to adjust its position, but lift it straight up from the icing and shift it to the appropriate place. Follow this same procedure if the stencil must be moved to complete the sprayed design with additional colors.

When the stencil is in the correct position, the decorator will be ready to spray the first color. He should be careful to hold the airbrush as nearly vertical as the instrument will allow, so that the mist will not spray under the stencil. Bottle fed models cannot be tipped to as extreme an angle as can the reservoir fed airbrushes— bottles, especially if they are overfilled, may leak when they are tipped too much.

SHIFT THE STENCIL

If the design is more complex, the stencil must be moved before the design can be completed. Carefully lift and shift the stencil to the correct place and finish spraying the pattern. The stencils and the nylon net should be blotted after each use so that the residue of colors is not transferred to the icing on the next cake to be stenciled. To do this, lay a smooth, dampened soft towel on the workbench beside the airbrush, set the stencil or screen on the cloth, and blot it with another damp cloth on top.

54

STRIPES, CHECKS, AND PLAIDS

A colorful variety of striped and checkered designs can be easily sprayed with a "stripe" stencil and with one or two colors. For a very unique and mystifying effect, the decorator can use this same stencil to produce an assortment of colorful plaids. One color is first used to spray criss-cross checks, then the stencil must be shifted half a stripe and sprayed with a second color. A third color can be applied over this design after the stencil is removed from the cake.

SILHOUETTES

Attractive silhouettes of any shape or size can be sprayed on a cake to add to the decorating theme. Antique cars, hearts, ovals, horseshoes, and shamrocks are only a few of the possibilities. In some cases, the silhouette can be the whole decoration, requiring only a written greeting to complete the cake's design. An interesting effect can also be achieved by using a heart or oval and spraying around it to produce a negative silhouette.

USE A STENCIL TO REDUCE THE DECORATING AREA

Stencils are particularly useful on cakes that are larger than the usual quarter-sheet size. Since larger cakes generally require more decoration, one can save time and reduce the amount of icing that is normally needed by stenciling a pattern to produce a frame like the one in this illustration. Depending on the choice of stencils, one can use color for the frame, or he can spray inside the design to leave a white frame around the smaller decorating area. A border around the design and at the edge of the cake will finish the frame. leaving only the smaller, center background

STENCILED SCENIC BACKGROUNDS

Beautiful scenic backgrounds can be produced for almost any type of sporting event or for any sort of vacation theme. If the cake is for a boating or camping enthusiast, the "wilderness" scene is ideal. This mountain-lake stencil is an especially helpful aid for those decorators who find it difficult to create their own artistic scenes.

With only minor changes, this scene can be altered to provide a perfect background for swimming, fishing, water skiing, or almost any other marine activity. When the use of close-up figures might be more desirable, part of the scene can be replaced with a larger lake. To do this, the decorator must airbrush only the distant mountains and trees; then, he should remove the stencil from the cake and complete the scene by spraying the entire foreground portion like a reflective lake.

By this same method, the decorator can replace the larger lake with a green meadow that would be suitable for baseball, soccer, football, or even for a picnic scene.

One of these "Bon Voyage" cakes, with its pounding surf and its palm trees silhouetted before a sunset sky, will make all the guests at the party envious of the south sea island vacationer. The "Hawaii" stencil makes this a background that cannot be rivaled by any other.

Without piping extra palm trees, or grass huts and hula dancers, the decorator can use this scene as a finished cake; with those additions, he can produce a cake that will tell a complete story.

The trees and all the land masses are sprayed with black. Then rainbow hues are misted over the sky and sea. The top third of the sky is blue; the bottom third, pink. The pink mist should be streaked in a zig-zag pattern upward through the sky, and also should be sprayed across the very top edge of the blue to create a violet overcast. Yellow is then airbrushed to fill in the center area, and to slightly overlap the blue and pink hues. The water's colors, being a reflection, should be airbrushed with the same colors in a pattern exactly reversed from those in the sky.

AIRBRUSHED THREE-DIMENSIONAL LANDSCAPES

With practice a decorator can produce a sculptured landscape that will look like a miniaturized section of land that could have been lifted straight out of one of America's national parks. Almost every detail, right down to the remarkable texture of the shrubs and trees, can be created with cake and icing. The addition of rock-candy boulders and cinnamon-sugar sand will almost convince the observer that he is viewing the real thing. The beauty of it all is that the decorator can sculpture the whole cake, cover it just with white icing, and can spray it with the appropriate colors in little more time than it would take for him to prepare and to decorate an average cake of the same size.

Fill and ice an ordinary sheet cake of whatever size is necessary to provide the customer with the right number of servings. Because extra cake must be used to build the mountains and hills, the completed sculpture will serve more guests than would a sheet cake of comparable size.

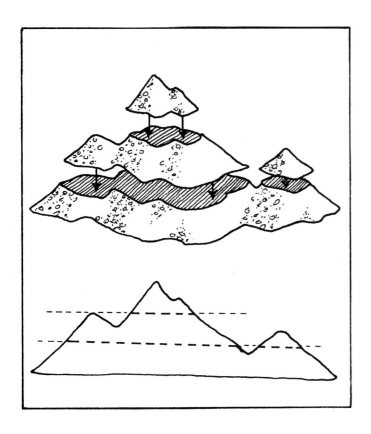

Use a sharp knife to cut a scrap from the same type cake as the iced sheet, and shape it into a cone. This cone will form the peak of the largest mountain. Set this cone-shaped piece onto a bigger scrap of cake and carve from it the lower hills and the base for the larger mountain. A third layer of cake may be required to produce adequate height for the mountain range. Use the same method for making any lone foothills on the landscape.

Set the layers together, using icing to hold them in place, and situate the mountains on the iced sheet cake. Use this opportunity to carve any lakes, streams, or valleys that seem desirable. The decorator should now make sure that the miniature scene is trimmed exactly to the shape and size that will project the most realistic image possible before he attempts to ice the completed sculpture.

Pipe bands of icing over the sculptured contours of the cake, using an "all purpose edging tip" (see CHAPTER I — MATERIALS AND EQUIPMENT). Use a small bowl knife or a palette knife to smooth the mountains and to create texture wherever it will add to the realism of the scene. Grass-like texture can be achieved by pulling the knife straight up from the icing to produce a stippled effect.

Cover any lakes or streams with a thin layer of piping jell, and the cake is ready to be airbrushed with the appropriate colors. Spray the main portion of the land with

green and add accents of brown. In this stage, be careful not to color either the snowy peaks or the piping jell surfaces. From the right side of the cake, hold the airbrush low, and spray yellow mist across the green hills and fields—this will create realistic highlights. Move the airbrush to the left side and spray a blue mist across the cake to produce life-like shadows. For darker shadows in some areas, overspray the blue with violet. LIGHT shadows and highlights should also be misted on the snow-covered peaks. Spray details like the water and the shorelines last.

60

The trees and bushes are sculptured from cake. Use a cake that is very porous so that the bits of cake will have a spongy texture which resembles real foliage. With sharp scissors, cut irregular clusters of little cones. Make the cones of different heights so that each cluster looks like a real clump of trees. Cut single trees for some of the landscaping, and use the remaining crumbs of cake for random shrubs and bushes. Push the trees and bushes into position on the iced cake, and spray them green, with yellow highlights and blue shadows.

After the trees are colored, the decorator may add cinnamon-sugar for sandy beaches, or for freshly cultivated soil. Tiny sesame seeds can be placed on a contoured roadway to simulate gravel and can be sprayed grey for greater realism. Rock candy can be used to create large boulders, and the land can be sectioned off with icing fences. The decorator can use his imagination to add any special details that he may desire.

LEARN TO USE COMPOSITION

Cake decorating is a part of *art*, a medium in its own right, just as are painting, architectural designing, sculpturing, or any of the other visual arts. Through the relentless inquiry born of a desire to communicate beauty and harmony to others, the experts in these fields of art throughout history have left guideposts and tested theories to follow. These theories are the blueprints for today's visual arts, and therefore are essential in cake decorating if the decorator is to create a desirable composition.

Usually the cakes will be rectangular sheets, ovals, or the traditional round layers. All three lend themselves to the basic principles of composition. The only exception to these rules would possibly be the symmetrical style decoration such as on the wedding cake, which will be discussed later in this chapter.

Consider the top of the cake as a piece of paper on which a picture is about to be drawn. Consider, too, the subject of the decoration, whether it is to be a pictorial landscape or a floral arrangement. No line or mass should bisect the middle of the cake, either vertically or horizontally. It should be above or below or to either side of dead center.

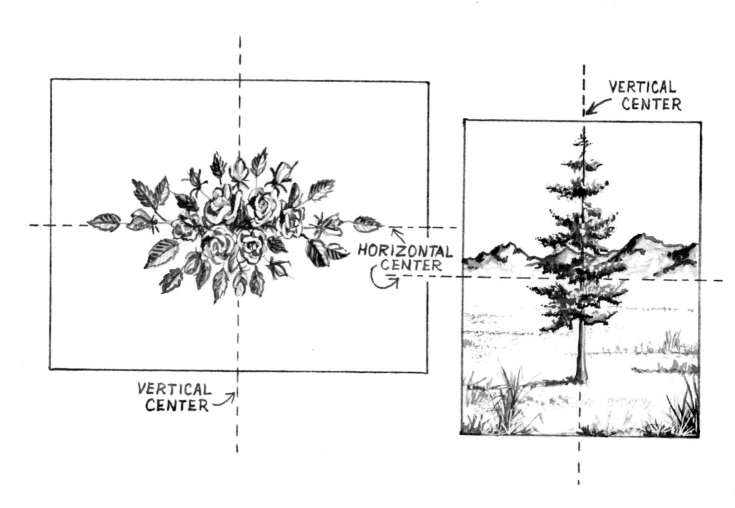

These illustrations are exaggerated examples of poor composition. Equally poor composition may occur if the artist does not use good judgment or if he fails to plan his picture carefully.

62

Experience shows that objects of similar size are more interesting if they appear in odd-numbered lots. Trees of about the same size should be placed in numbers of three, five, etc., or the artist should use a single trunk by itself.

POOR COMPOSITION

The base of the mountain in this illustration is centered both vertically and horizontally. Furthermore, the tree trunks forming the landscape are examples of even-numbered objects that are too similar in size.

GOOD COMPOSITION

The mountain, as the primary background object, is well to one side of the vertical center, and the horizon line is lower than the horizontal center of the picture. The trees, although they are the same type, are repeated in uneven numbers and are of dissimilar sizes so that they help to create interest and a feeling of depth.

POOR COMPOSITION

Because of the positions in which the two buildings are situated, they appear to be too nearly the same size. The horizon line is centered in the picture, and a mountain peak rises at the middle of the horizon.

GOOD COMPOSITION

By altering the position of the buildings within the landscape, the barn is moved to the foreground, making the scene more interesting. The subjects of this scene are exactly the same as those in the illustration above. By showing them from a different viewpoint, the artist has created a more satisfying composition. Undoubtedly any observer would find viewing this scene to be a much more pleasurable experience.

Incidental hills, rocks, trees, etc., en masse in the background of a scene should be considered as one object. Such masses fall under the same treatment as would a single tree or mountain because they are usually so distant that one cannot see details and often cannot distinguish individual objects.

HORIZON LINE

The horizon line in any picture is the line at which the sky and level land appear to meet. The key word is "level." If there are mountains or other obstacles that obscure the horizon, one must sometimes imagine its approximate position.

If the observer is in a normal standing position amidst a fairly level scene, the horizon line will appear to be a little above the center of the picture.

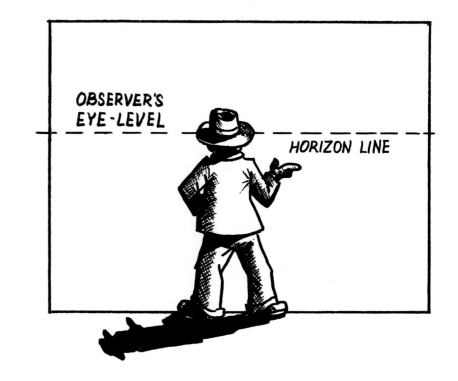

If the observer is sitting or kneeling, the horizon line will be below the center. Its placement will be in direct relationship to the level of the viewer's eyes.

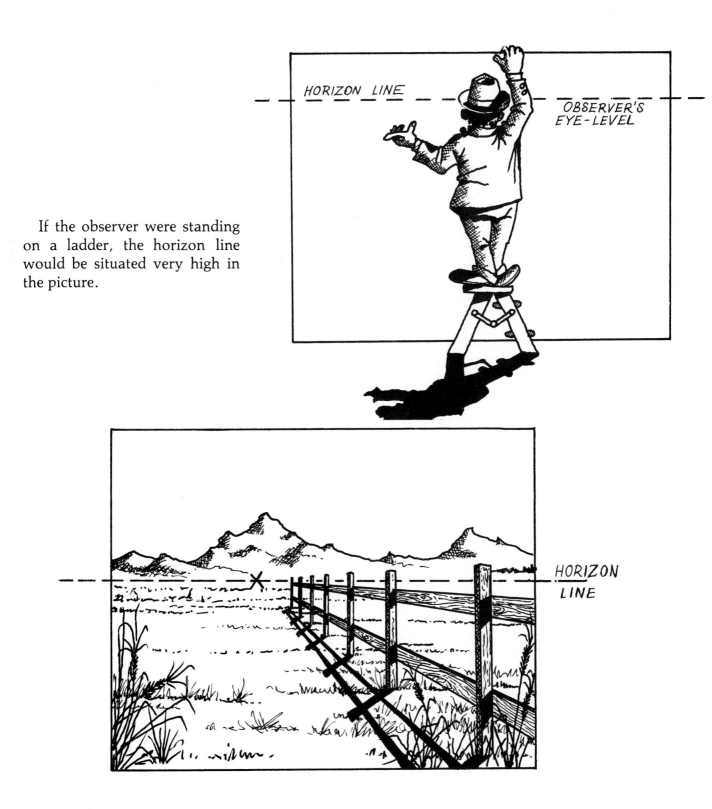

If the observer were standing on a ladder, the horizon line would be situated very high in the picture.

PERSPECTIVE

Perspective is an illusion in which equal-sized objects will appear to be smaller or larger depending on whether they are far from or very close to the observer's point of view. For example, imagine lines of fence posts or of telephone poles that seem to get smaller and smaller until they nearly disappear, or picture a railroad track that seems to grow narrower in the distance.

Fence posts in the foreground appear to be separated by much greater margins than those in the distance, and as the train track narrows, the ties seem closer and closer together. This same illusion of depth can be created on cakes by the use of perspective.

The only way to benefit from the study of perspective is to practice many hours. Practice enough that this becomes natural. Obviously a decorator will not be able to draw all the necessary guide lines on the surface of an iced cake, therefore, the elements of perspective must be studied until they become almost habit or instinct.

LEARN WITH PENCIL AND PAPER

To read this course on perspective without applying its concepts, lesson-by-lesson, by drawing with pencil and paper, will be of little value. Use a standard drawing board or smooth piece of hardboard, two or three times the size of the drawing paper. A very sharp pencil with a fairly soft lead will be best, and it would be advisable to have a good eraser handy. Fasten the paper to the drawing board with masking tape so that it will stay properly aligned. Masking tape can be removed without tearing the paper and will adhere well to most surfaces without peeling off before one is ready.

OBSERVER'S POINT OF VIEW

Many times throughout this chapter, reference will be made to the observer's point of view, or to just "the observer." This point occurs at the exact center of the horizon line. It will help if the artist keeps in mind that he is the observer, as he draws the various objects in the picture. With each object, the artist must take into account its position, its form, and its size as it is related to his point of view. The observer's position must remain stationary for the whole picture.

If the object is a box, sitting on the ground or the floor, below and to the side of the observer, one would see the top, the front, and perhaps one of the sides (depending on the angle of the box).

If the object is an overhanging porch or balcony surrounded by a low wall above the observer, only the underside of the balcony, the front wall, and maybe one side wall will be visible. Always remember that *every* object within a scene is relative to the observer. In essence, no matter where each item is located in the picture, the artist must situate it exactly as it should appear from a single point of view.

BEGIN WITH ACCURATE CONCEPTS

The artist must carefully imagine how each subject is situated and exactly which planes of that object will be visible as he begins to draw it. If it is too difficult to imagine exactly how a particular object will appear, set up a model in a position comparable to the subject being drawn and sketch from that.

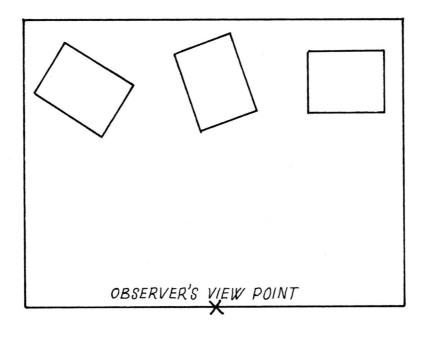

OBSERVER'S VIEW POINT
X

To get a better picture in mind, draw a rectangle to represent the floor of a room, and place small rectangles to represent boxes sitting at different angles across one side of the room. Midway on the wall opposite the side with the boxes, mark an X to indicate the position of the observer.

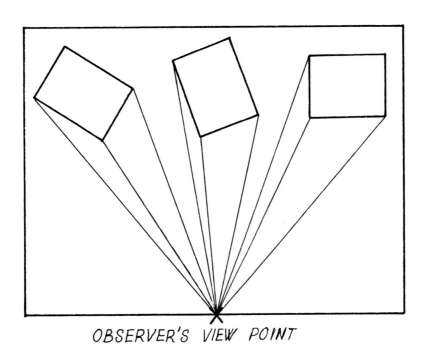

OBSERVER'S VIEW POINT

Select any of the small rectangles and draw light lines from the X to those corners which are exposed to the observer. This will help to illustrate just how much of each side of that box will be visible to the observer.

OBSERVER'S PLANE

Think first of a person sitting, looking at a particular view. If it were possible to view this situation from above—a bird's eye view, so to speak—one would see the observer and the top view of all of the objects within that scene. Think of a line drawn across directly in front of the observer to separate him from the rest of the scene. This line represents the observer's plane, i.e., the surface of a picture. Some of the objects in the scene may be parallel to this plane, revealing only their front surfaces to the observer, while others may be at angles to the observer's point of view. If the object is at an angle to the observer, he will be able to see two surfaces (the front and one side), and these surfaces will be affected by the illusion of perspective.

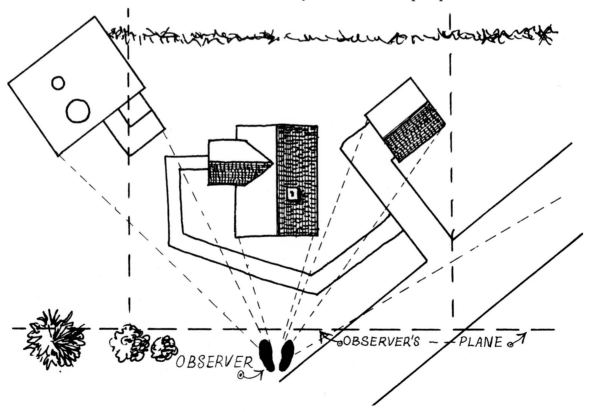

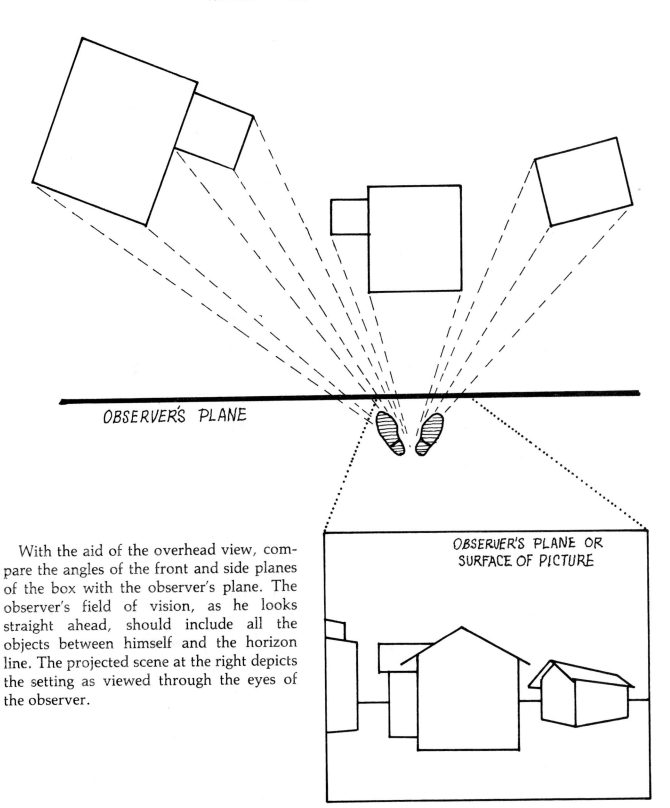

HORIZON LINE

OBSERVER'S PLANE

OBSERVER'S PLANE OR SURFACE OF PICTURE

With the aid of the overhead view, compare the angles of the front and side planes of the box with the observer's plane. The observer's field of vision, as he looks straight ahead, should include all the objects between himself and the horizon line. The projected scene at the right depicts the setting as viewed through the eyes of the observer.

UNDERSTANDING TWO POINT PERSPECTIVE

Three-dimensional perspective requires the use of two or more vanishing points. These vanishing points can be located anywhere on the horizon line. They represent the points where the parallel lines of any object in the picture would appear to meet if they were extended to the horizon line.

Earlier, this text explored the overhead view of objects—a concept that took into account only the top plane. Two point perspective takes into consideration the top or bottom and the sides of an object, and depicts both depth and dimension. The simplest form to use for this study is a box.

This hypothetical overhead view includes the subject, the observer's plane, and the horizon line.

Lines, from the front and from the visible side of a box, that are extended to the horizon line, provide the locations for the vanishing points. The respective positions of these vanishing points are directly dependent on the angle of the boxes. Since the vanishing points can be located by drawing lines from the angled side and front planes of a given box, it must be allowed that one can reverse the process to draw a box from given vanishing points. This is shown in the projected view in the lower part of the illustration.

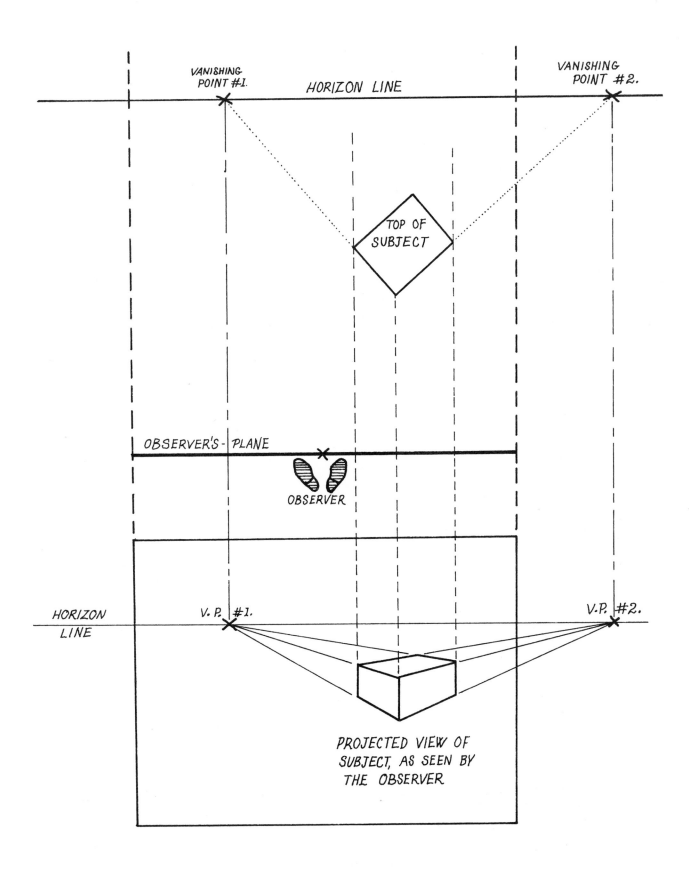

VANISHING POINT #1.

VANISHING POINT #2.

HORIZON LINE

TOP OF SUBJECT

OBSERVER'S - PLANE

OBSERVER

HORIZON LINE

V. P. #1.

V.P. #2.

PROJECTED VIEW OF SUBJECT, AS SEEN BY THE OBSERVER

LEARN TO DRAW WITH TWO POINT PERSPECTIVE

Locate a rectangular piece of paper near the left side of a drawing board and secure each of its corners with tape. For this practice, place a horizon line a little above the center of the paper. Extend the line beyond the right edge of the paper onto the drawing board.

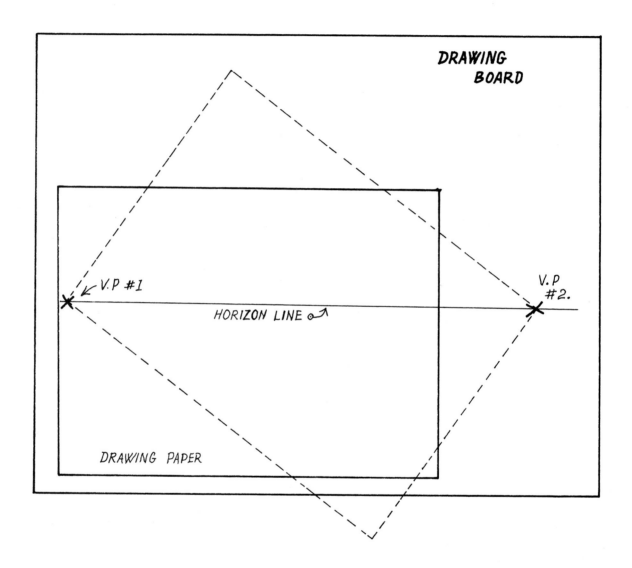

Select the first vanishing point near the left side of the paper on the horizon line. The second vanishing point will be placed on that portion of the horizon line which extends onto the drawing board. To locate this second vanishing point, measure the paper diagonally. Use this measurement to determine the distance between the first and second vanishing points. This method will work accurately enough for the needs of most decorators.

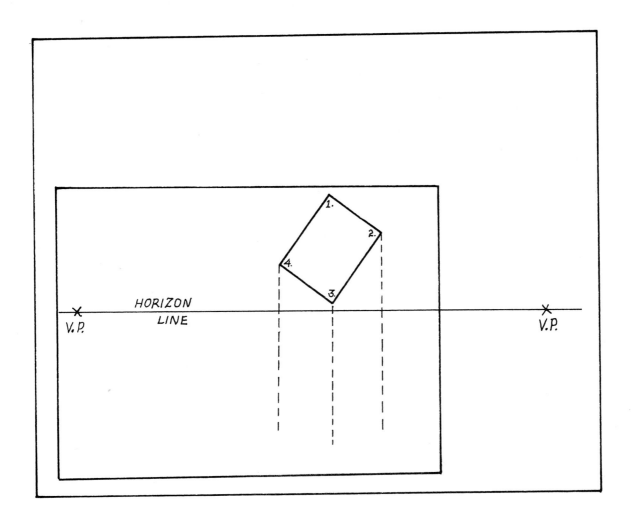

Draw a rectangle or square to represent the top of a box, above the horizon line, between the two vanishing points. The rectangle should be drawn at an angle to the horizon line.

Just inside the rectangle, number the corners clockwise, beginning at the top corner, 1, 2, 3, and 4. Now draw dotted lines from Corners 2, 3, and 4 to the bottom of the paper. Be sure to keep all of the lines straight and parallel to the paper's edge.

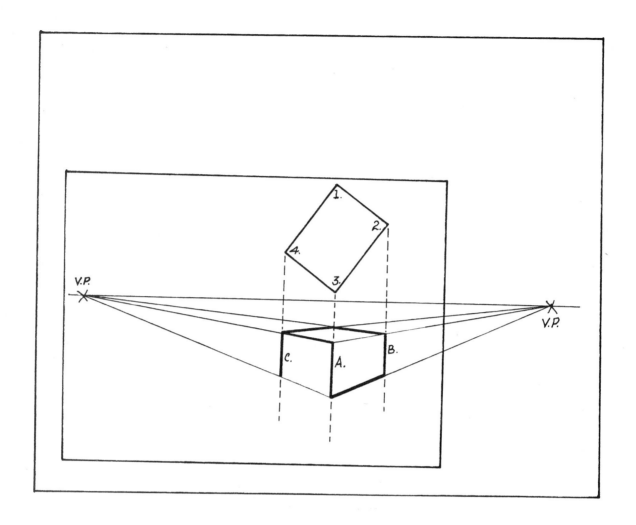

The next step will be to reproduce a box in the lower portion of the drawing paper. Beginning about two inches below the horizon line, draw over Line Number 3 to make a solid line about the same length as the shortest side on the rectangle above. This segment should be identified as Line A, and will represent the leading edge of the box. From the top of Line A draw a *light* perspective line to each vanishing point. Do the same from the bottom of Line A. Darken that part of Line Number 2 which lies between the light perspective lines and identify it as Line B. Fill in the light perspective lines between Line A and Line B to complete one plane of the box. Draw in Line Number 4 at the left and label that segment Line C. Filling in the perspective lines between Line C and Line A will create a second plane. Beginning at the top of Line B, draw a *light* perspective line to the vanishing point at the left of the paper. Now, draw another *light* perspective line from the top of Line C to the vanishing point at the right. From the point where these two lines converge, to the tops of Lines B and C, darken the lines to form the third plane and to complete the box.

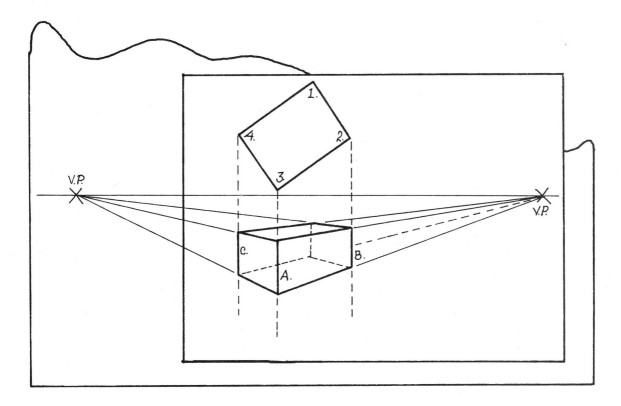

The box just completed shows its top and two sides. Following the same formula, boxes can be drawn in perspective anywhere on a paper, using similar locations for the two vanishing points. Remember that the drawings in the space above the horizon line will reveal the bottoms of the boxes rather than the tops, because these boxes will be above the observer's point of view. Therefore, in the last step before drawing the third and final plane of the box, one should draw the light perspective lines from the bottom of Lines B and C, rather than from the top.

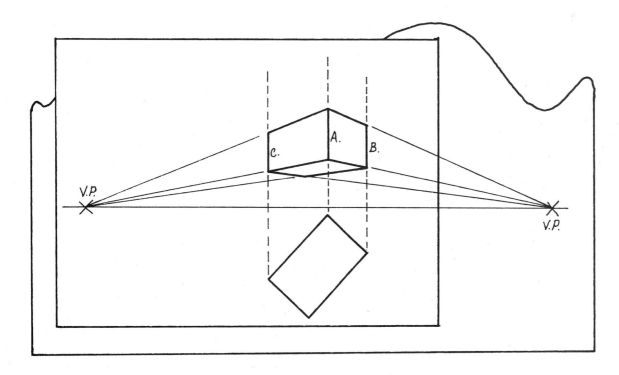

80

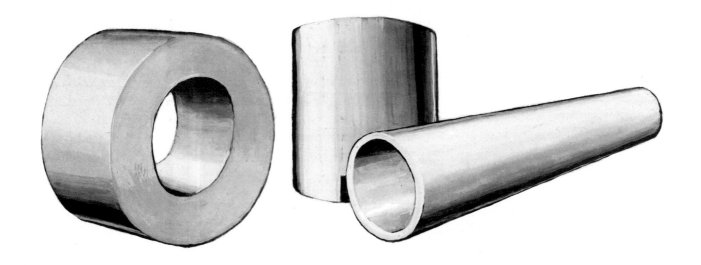

CYLINDERS IN PERSPECTIVE

Become thoroughly familiar with the mechanics of perspective before attempting anything other than boxes. Drawing objects with curved edges is much more difficult than drawing boxes, but the same rules apply. The end of a cylinder, when viewed from an angle, will appear to be oval rather than round. When such an object is enclosed in a transparent box, it is easier to understand how its shape is affected by perspective. By the same token, a cylinder is more easily drawn in perspective if the artist begins by drawing a box of proper proportions to fit the position and space to be occupied by that cylinder. The center of any exposed plane of a box can be pin-pointed by criss-crossing that plane with diagonal lines from corner to corner. The point where the two lines intersect marks the perspective center.

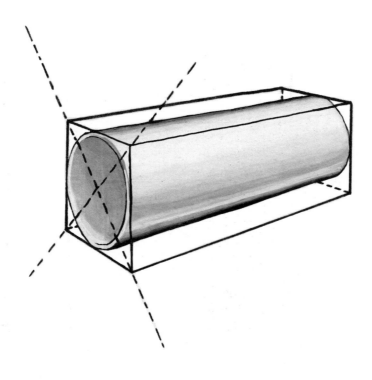

Picture a cylinder lying on its side. When viewed from above, the silhouette of this cylinder looks like a rectangle similar to the top plane of a rectangular box. The objectives of this exercise will be, first, to draw a transparent box and, second, to draw a cylinder within the boundaries of that box.

Set up a drawing paper with two vanishing points on the horizon line. Draw a rectangle at an angle above the horizon line. Then, by following the same procedures that were outlined in the previous exercises, draw a box, in perspective, below the horizon line. This box must, however, be drawn with the extra lines that are necessary to reveal all six of its planes. Use dotted lines to define the edges of those planes which ordinarily would not be visible if the box were a solid form.

Before proceeding to the next part of this exercise, erase all traces of the *light* perspective guide lines that were used to draw the box. These lines, if not erased, will cause unnecessary confusion. Do not erase the vanishing points.

The small, front plane of this box will become the front end of the cylinder. Locate the perspective center of this plane with corner-to-corner diagonal lines. This center point, where the diagonals cross, will be the axis of the cylinder. Draw a vertical line through that axis and another line to bisect the plane horizontally. The horizontal dividing line must be in perspective with the top and bottom lines of the plane, so locate it correctly by using a straight edge from the vanishing point to the axis. These two dividing lines, where they cross the outer edges of the front plane, mark the positions where the edges of the cylinder's wall will touch the walls of the box.

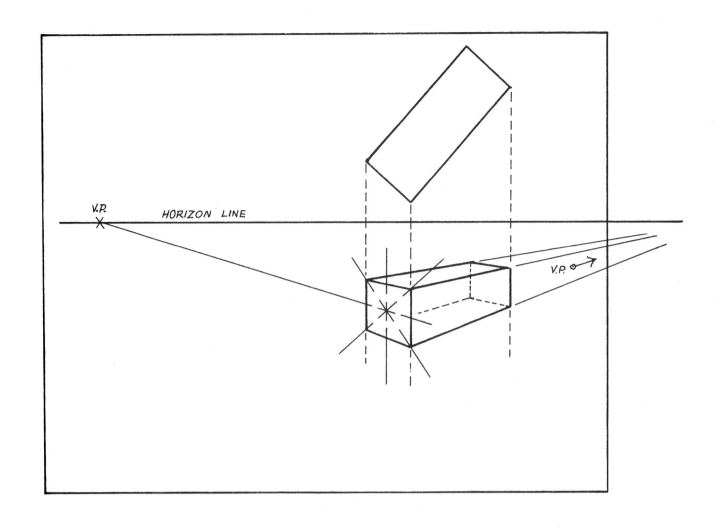

HORIZON LINE

V.P.

V.P.

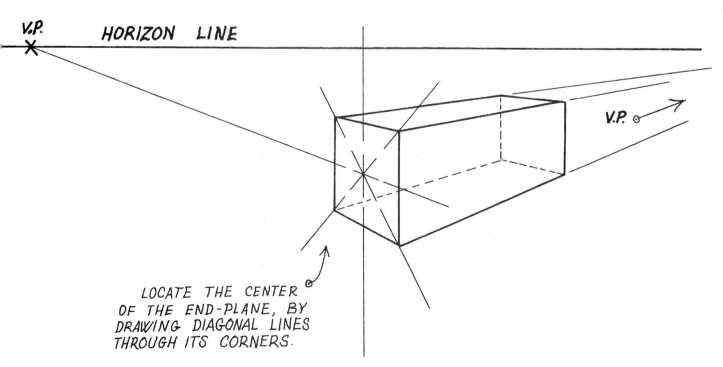

V.P.

HORIZON LINE

V.P.

LOCATE THE CENTER
OF THE END-PLANE, BY
DRAWING DIAGONAL LINES
THROUGH ITS CORNERS.

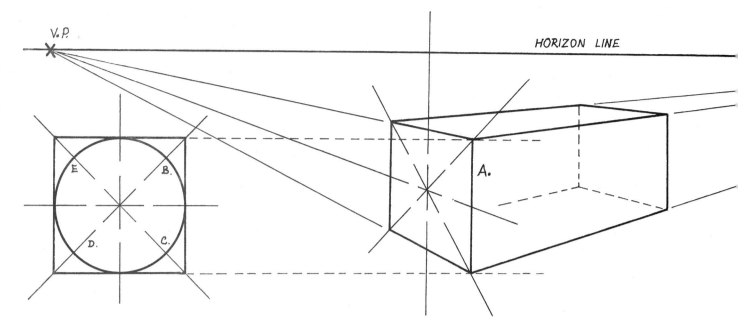

Draw a projected plane. The projected plane, adjacent to the box, is a PERFECT SQUARE; the length of each of its sides is equal to the length of the leading edge of the box (Line A). Do not draw the dotted parallel lines for locating the projected plane. The dotted lines in this illustration are for reference only, to indicate the correct placement and size of the square.

Divide the square into eight wedges to coincide with the divisions in the end of the box. Draw a circle to reveal four specific "contact points" on the diagonal lines and label them clockwise, B, C, D and E.

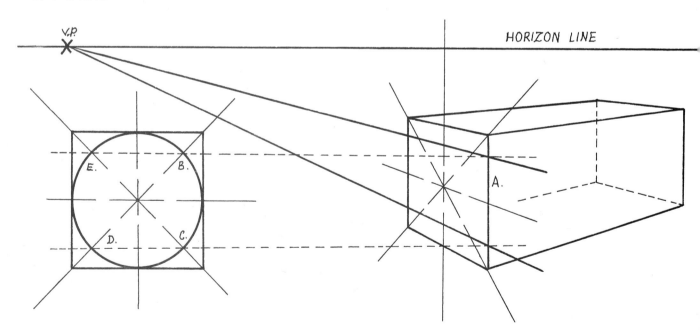

This illustration shows the two levels at which Line A must be divided. These levels are indicated by the parallel, dotted lines that extend from points B and C, over and through Line A. Use a straight edge and mark the positions on Line A where it is intersected by the dotted lines.

Now, use these two points on Line A; draw a perspective line from each, through the end of the box, to the vanishing point on the left side of the horizon line.

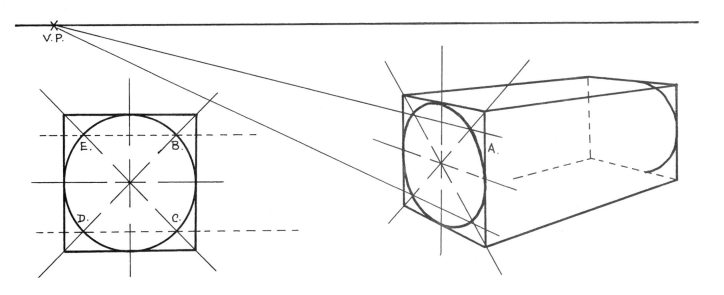

The intersections, where the last two perspective lines cross the diagonals on the front plane of the box, mark the four contact points for the cylinder's wall. A curved line drawn through all eight contact points will produce a perspective view of the front rim of the cylinder. Use this completed view as a guide to draw a matching curve at the other end of the box to form the back plane of the cylinder.

This freehand approach to drawing the far end of the cylinder will be sufficient for most cake decorating needs. Technically, however, it is possible to draw this plane by the same process as was used in the previous exercise.

Draw two lines to form the sides of the cylinder's wall, and erase the lighter guide lines to complete the drawing in proper perspective.

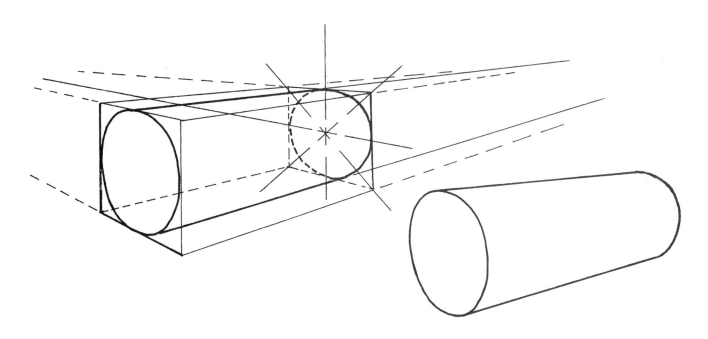

This exercise, with the first reading, will be difficult to comprehend. With their first attempts, most students tend to be overwhelmed with the mechanical process. However, when the instructions are reread and when the student attempts to draw in accordance with the directions, his comprehension will greatly improve. Repeated practice of the foregoing exercise should provide the necessary experience so that, eventually, a person will be able to draw cylindrical forms in perspective without needing to use the mechanical guide lines.

The principal reason for learning the accurate shaping for cylinders is for the decorator to be able, with sufficient practice, to draw wheels, tin cans, and the like as they should appear from different points of view. One should be able to draw, freehand, such shapes so that they will appear to be in perspective and will reflect their accurate positions and dimensions in a picture.

USE THE ELEMENTS OF COMPOSITION AND PERSPECTIVE TO DRAW A PICTURE

Notice how this soup tureen is composed of sections from spheres, cones, and cylinders.

This barn makes use of box and cylindrical shapes. The roof of the silo is a simple cone.

Some objects require extra shaping and rounding off, but are basically simple forms.

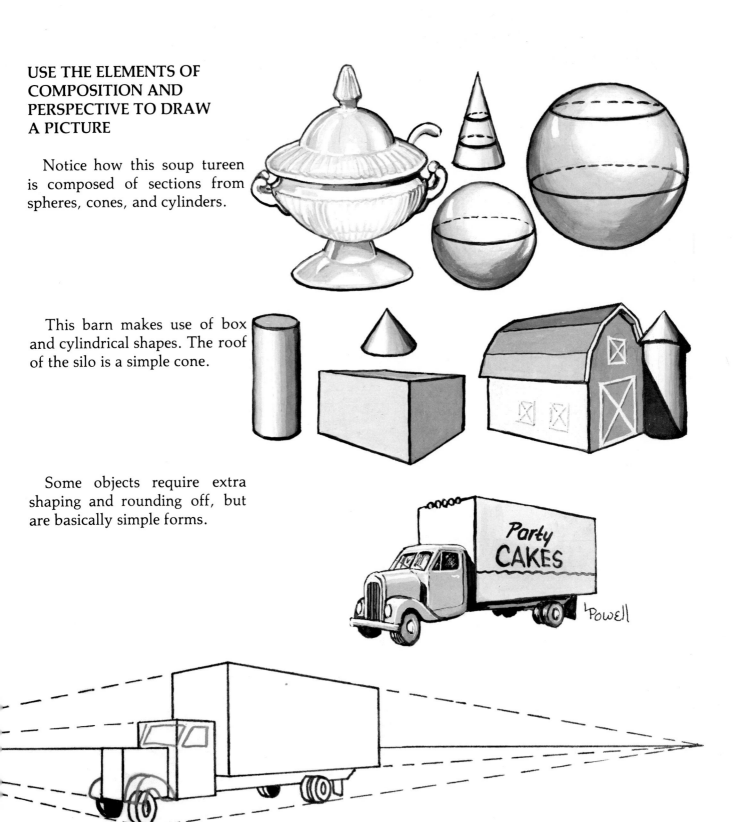

Most objects can be likened in form to a cylinder, a box, a sphere, or a cone. With this concept it is possible to draw various forms, like buildings, cars, tables, etc., in perspective, using the one point or the two point perspective system as a guide.

ONE POINT PERSPECTIVE

Forms with principally one plane, such as roads, rivers, fences, and railroad tracks, are treated like one of the planes of a box. A flat surface such as a road is like the top of the box, and the fence is more like the side of the box.

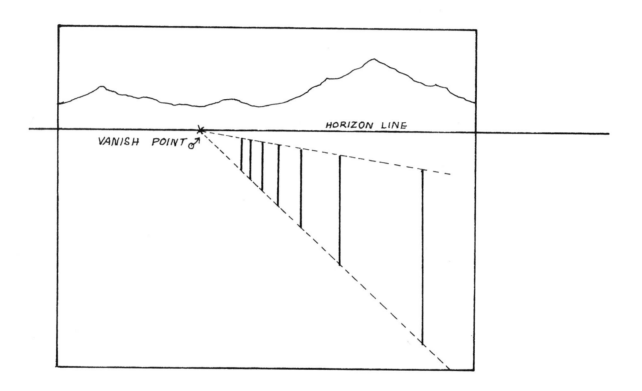

Prepare another paper with the horizon line above the center, only this time, place a single vanishing point somewhere on the left side of the line. Now, draw a vertical line, to represent a fence post, on the far right-hand side of the paper. Let the line extend upward from near the bottom of the paper to a point just below the horizon line. Remember the horizon line is eye-level, so the position of this post would indicate that the fence is about chest-high to the observer.

Draw a dotted perspective line from the top of the post to the vanishing point on the horizon line, and another from the bottom of the post to the same point. The distance between these two lines will reveal the height for each post. Now place the second post behind the first. Continue adding the rest of the posts, keeping in mind that all succeeding posts must be closer and closer together.

To practice spacing fence posts with more mechanical accuracy, draw a light diagonal line from the top of the first post through the center of the second, extending it to the lower perspective line. The bottom of the third post should be located at the intersection of this diagonal and the lower perspective line. Each post, in turn, may be located in the same manner.

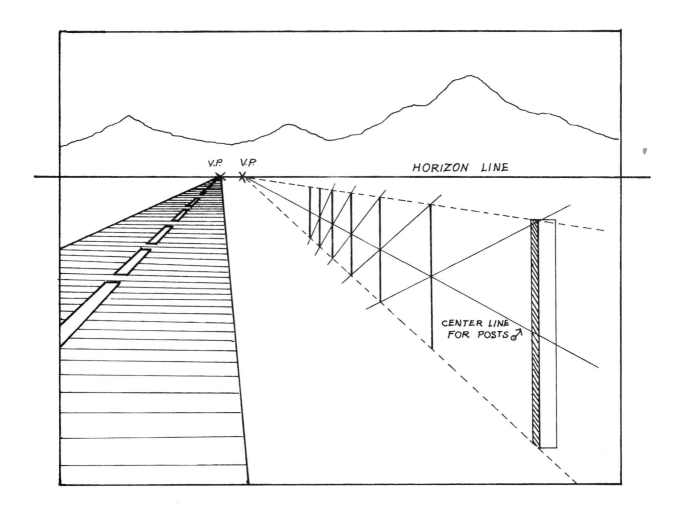

A straight road running alongside this fence would use a single vanishing point in near proximity to the one for the fence, depending on the distance between the edge of the road and the fence line. If, however, the road runs zig-zag through the picture, the angle of its edges must be determined by a new vanishing point on the horizon line each time the road bends to a new direction. In this case the picture determines the placement and the number of vanishing points which the artist must use.

ONE AND TWO POINT PERSPECTIVE COMBINED

Occasionally, the composition of a scene will require more than two vanishing points. Using the system with only two vanishing points assumes that all of the objects within that picture are sitting at exactly the same angle. Try to recall the overhead view of the scene which explained the observer's plane and remember that the objects in that scene are not necessarily arranged so that the line which forms the front side of one of the objects is at the same angle as the front line of the next. Occasionally it will be necessary for the decorator to compose a picture to reveal this random sort of arrangement within a scene. To turn anything to an angle which is different from that of another object in the scene, one must set up individual vanishing points accordingly.

In this scene, for example, the house is situated one way, while both the fence and the road are situated at different angles. The house was drawn with two point perspective; the fence and each angle of the road were produced by the one point method.

90

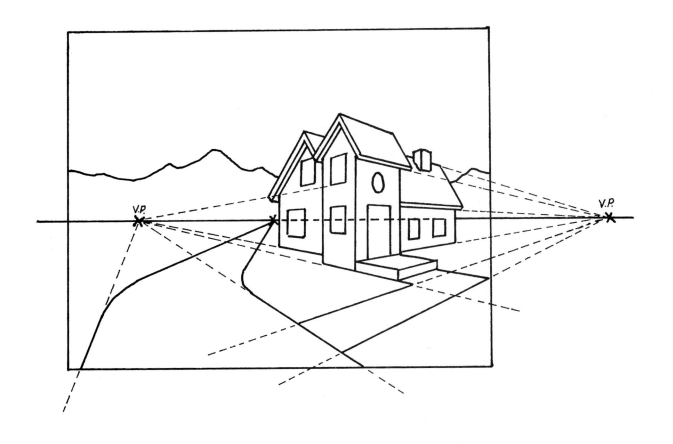

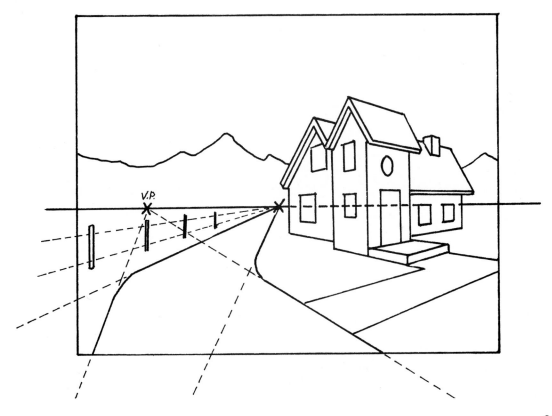

COMPOSITION OF FLORAL DECORATIONS

Composition, as it applies to floral decorations, is concerned primarily with the shape of the arrangement and its position on the cake. Each decorator may choose the formation that best suits his taste. Perhaps a trip to the local flower shops would be worthwhile, as most florists are usually happy to show sample books and catalogs with various styles and ideas. The crescent-shaped bouquet is popular and is generally preferred by this writer.

With flowers, keep in mind the importance of variation in sizes and in colors. Make certain that the open roses, or whatever flowers are used, range from smaller blossoms to larger more mature blooms. Of course, there should be a pleasant number of buds to fill out the shape of the arrangement.

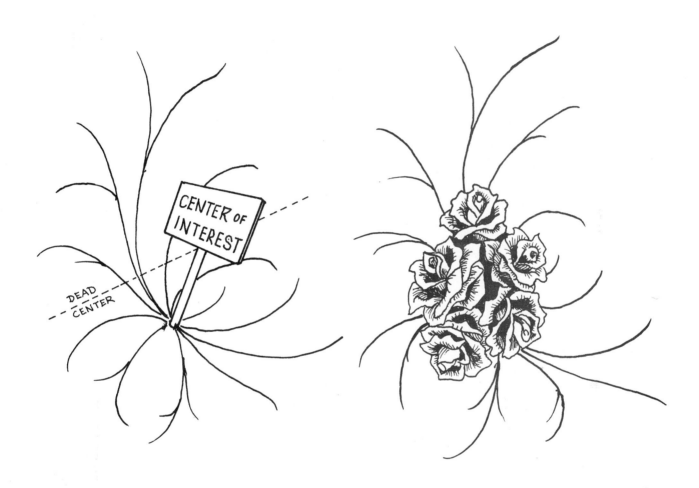

First arrange the stems in lines that express whatever shape has been chosen for the floral piece. Situate the bulk of the larger blossoms either above or below dead center on the stem arrangement, and let this point be the center of interest. Aim each blossom away from this point. The nice thing about the crescent arrangement is the fact that, once the viewer's eye falls on the center of interest, the lines of the crescent carry his attention on around the whole cake and back again to the main cluster of blossoms in the arrangement. This is part of the trick of good composition—to keep the eye in motion within the boundaries of the cake's borders. Make the decorations so attractive that the viewer will want to look and look until he hasn't missed a detail.

94

Leaves, their type, and their arrangement, are very important on a cake. Not only must the mass of blossoms be the focal point at first glance, but each bud and cluster of leaves should, in its own way, add to the design as the eye of the viewer returns to get that good look at the whole design. The exact point of interest is at the center of the cluster of full blooms. *Each blossom should face away from the center of interest* so that the bouquet radiates from that area. The leaves around that cluster should also radiate from the same point.

The leaves in the rest of the arrangement may radiate from the single buds so that they too may become secondary points of interest. With these properly placed, the addition of a few more leaves to fill in the blank areas will complete a very pleasing and satisfying picture.

It is important to choose a type of leaf that fits the flowers. *Don't decorate with rose leaves for everything.* Use long, slender leaves for daffodils and carnations, wide boat-shaped leaves for dogwood, and rounded flat leaves for violets; try to be aware of shapes that match the blossoms and that enhance the decoration.

Earlier in this chapter a reference was made to wedding cakes and, more specifically, to their symmetrical form of decoration. This formal style of decorating has little regard for the rules of composition which the student formerly learned to use for an overall cake design. Instead, these elements must be applied to isolated segments of the design. Each part must be treated as an individual composition. Whatever pattern the decorator selects must be repeated around the whole perimeter of the cake to form a design that could be likened to that which one might see inside a kaleidoscope. The intricately beautiful border work might simply be considered as an elaborate means of applying texture to the background of the composition.

A cluster of flowers and buds in small bouquets around the cake is favored by this writer; however, many brides prefer a simpler design. Such a cluster of blossoms, and the leaves which accompany it, should receive the same attention and treatment as a floral arrangement which the decorator would use in the composition on a regular decorated cake.

If only one flower is used at each point in the design, it should be aimed outward from the center of the cake so that the viewer sees the open face of the blossom. The leaves should radiate from underneath, so as to point directly away from the center of the flower.

It is fine, occasionally, to use this type of decoration on round or oval layers, or on sheet cakes for variety. Consider using a symmetrical design on those cakes which are ordered for more formal celebrations such as bridal showers or anniversaries. Sometimes it will add just the right touch of majesty to the occasion; after all, isn't that the main purpose of the decorated cake?

THE IMPORTANCE OF ARTISTIC AWARENESS

The success of the decorator to recreate the realism of a scene requires more than the study of any book. It depends on his ability to train his eyes and his mind to perceive nature's most inconspicuous details.

Like any other form of art, cake decorating requires that the artist constantly must maintain an AWARENESS of everything that exists. He must be able to see and to interpret accurately colors, textures, and shapes; he must be cognizant of such obscure details as depth, mood, and motion.

Everything is relative in proportion to another object, animal, or person. All things must be associated with familiar surroundings so that a particular theme or mood is established. The artist has a responsibility to make sure that the primary subject is accurately related to the other elements within a scene, to establish the compatability of those elements, and to adhere to a particular theme. This is the key to the creation of a comprehensive, uncluttered work of art.

Artistic awareness is not achieved by accident, it is only acquired through effort. The student must learn to look—really to LOOK—at everything in his presence. Man is given the ability to see, and he usually perceives in generalities; the artist is ordained to look, and to see the details within those generalities. Then he is charged with the responsibility of interpreting those details for the rest of mankind.

Most decorators have not learned to LOOK at their surroundings with that sense of responsibility which is common to almost all other artists. Therefore, it is of prime importance for the reader to learn from this time on, to analyze every element within his visual range. Only through this careful analysis can a decorator master the capacity to interpret and to recreate, accurately, the likeness of everything around him.

AWARENESS OF TREES

A good way for the student to begin to accumulate visual experience is for him to ask himself questions about details surrounding each specific object. Starting with "WHAT IS A TREE?" he can practice using this method of analysis and may then begin to apply this method to each thing with which he comes in contact.

What is the COLOR of a tree—is it green? IS IT GREEN, or is it really blue-green, or yellow-green, or gold, or rust, or orange, or is it silver? Does it even have foliage? and if it doesn't, what is the color of a tree? Is it brown, or grey, or white, or tan, or green, or is it black and white?

What is the SHAPE of a tree? Is it tall and like a cone, or is it short and round? What is the TEXTURE of a tree? Is it prickly, is it feathery, or is it puffy like a cloud? And what if? What if it has no foliage, is it gnarled, is it smooth, is it spiney, is it blistery? What is a tree?

What is its element? Does the tree grow in lush, green hill country? on sandy, rocky terrain? or, would one be more apt to find it in a damp, swampy region? Would it thrive in cool mountainous territory, or would it be more at home on a desert?

How would one go about drawing a tree—an oak, a palm, a maple, a pine, a birch? How would one draw a tree trunk? How would one draw a branch? How would one draw a leaf? What IS a tree?

EVERGREEN TREES

Evergreen trees retain their foliage the year around. Most prominent among the evergreen's variety are pines, cedars, sequoias, and firs. These trees are in evidence throughout many regions of the world, and so being, are important to the cake decorator's artistic awareness.

In their younger growth, they are shaped like cones. Often they grow in masses, and appear as feathery clumps when viewed from a distance. In composing a picture, these masses are treated as a single object.

In their later years, most evergreens lose much of their symmetrical, cone-shaped form and become more scraggly and irregular.

DECIDUOUS TREES

Unlike evergreen trees, deciduous trees are seasonal and they lose their leaves before winter each year. In springtime these trees don new foliage of colors that range from silvery-green to red-violet, not to mention gold, rust, orange, and almost every other hue in between. Trees of the green tones dominate, but even their green leaves turn to fiery colors with the emergence of autumn.

In the winter, deciduous trees stand as bare skeletons with only their graceful network of limbs and the texture and coloration of their bark. Some tree trunks are very smooth while others bear roughly textured bark, and some have distinctive colorations.

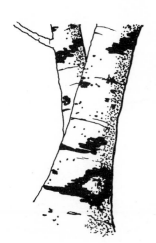

AWARENESS OF PEOPLE

If the student is concerned with figure piping, it is critically important for him to be aware of the abstract physical characteristics of human beings. He must be familiar with the shapes of faces and of their individual features. He must be cognizant of physical traits that are common to those people of a particular geographic or ethnic background. More importantly then, the student must analytically observe and note individual peculiarities such as the subject's age, his pigmentation, the color of his eyes, and the style, texture and color of his hair.

The portraits on these two pages are selected to illustrate general characteristics. Although they are not necessarily drawn from actual models, each is identifiable with a certain classification of people, and each causes an observer to immediately associate that face with a particular visual experience.

Each reader should begin his "awareness of people" training by carefully studying the four faces on these two pages. He should compare the characteristics of one with those of the other three faces, taking special notice of the shape of each nose, the texture and tone of each hair style, the facial structure, and the texture and tone of the skin. Using this experience as a guide, the decorator should then observe the people around him and should try to record mental pictures for future reference.

Although generalities can be adopted for whole classifications of people, it is extremely important that the reader should try to understand that each person is an individual. When doing a likeness of a particular person, one cannot generalize; he must treat each characteristic by itself. It is this separate identity that makes it possible and, at the same time, extremely difficult to draw, to paint, or to sculpture a portrait.

110

For some reason, certain faces seem to go with particular careers, just as do certain forms of dress. Thus, the decorator can type-cast his figure and often be fairly accurate in depicting a particular individual by just knowing the occupation. For instance, think of the average image conjured up in one's mind by these occupations: a bartender, a secretary, a neighborhood corner grocer, a librarian, a barber, and of course a baker. At just the thought of each of these roles, a particular image comes to mind. Now, don't forget the type of uniform or clothing that seems to fit the individual.

One would never make the obvious mistake of dressing a man in a tuxedo and top hat, only to have him carry a lunch bucket instead of a cane. A decorator must always be careful to maintain a specific theme. Realize that the recipient of the cake will be aware of inconsistencies if they exist, because the theme of the decoration depicts his or her particular occupation or hobby. This places extreme responsibility on the decorator, so he must know as much as possible about all occupations, sports, religions, clothing styles and other details. Know the tools and the symbols of their trades.

CHAPTER III
Borders, Pressure Control, and Wrist Action

Essential Mechanics of Cake Decorating
Basic Borders
String Work
Wedding Cake Designs

114

Borders, Pressure Control, and Wrist Action

Pressure control and wrist action should be described as the *mechanics* of cake decorating, and they can best be learned with the practice of the simple lines and shapes that are common to border designs. Learning to form borders and shapes with a decorating cone is vital to the education of any accomplished cake decorator. It is the key to the proper formation of flowers and figures, and to any other phase of cake art. At this point, the decorator could readily be likened to the young musician practicing his scales on the piano. Before the student has devoted nearly enough time to this phase, he will become tired and bored, and will want to get on to the more interesting and creative things like flowers and their arrangement; but, he must not allow himself to give up until he can execute all of the borders in this text without flaws. Smoothness and correct shape are vital, and even after his mechanical skill has been fairly well perfected, the student should return to this lesson and should practice some more.

For practicing most of these borders, the student should use either a Number 16 or a Number 18 star tip in a parchment decorating cone that is filled with plain white buttercream. Even though a cloth decorating bag might be more convenient, he should use parchment cones for practicing purposes because they allow better control of the pressure and give the decorator a precise feel of the icing and of how it is moving through the decorating tip. When the cone gets squeezed down beyond the remaining quarter of icing, the decorator must start over with a new cone; otherwise, the necessary control of the icing is lost when his hand is cramped around such a small surface. With practice one develops the ability to judge when to change cones; never should the student work with such a small amount of icing in the cone that it cannot be controlled to the finest degree. The top of the parchment cone must be twisted down tightly against the icing at all times, and the decorator should grip this twisted portion of the cone firmly within the cradle of this thumb and forefinger so as to allow his other three fingers to apply or to relax pressure according to the shape and the volume of icing that is to be extruded from the cone.

When doing any form of decorating, one must make the icing follow the decorating tip. The student should experiment with the angle of the cone and its relationship to the work surface, always to be certain that the icing is being pulled from, rather than being pushed into, the design. The icing must do exactly as the decorator directs at all times. Broken, wavy, or unwanted thick-and-thin lines indicate that the decorator lacks control over the icing. If these problems do occur, one should check the angle of the decorating cone and should make sure that it is not filled so full that the pressure cannot be accurately controlled. If the icing is coming out jerkily and in short blasts, even though constant pressure is being applied, he should squeeze some of the icing out of the decorating cone. This will relieve any air pockets that may have been formed when the cone was filled. If bursts of air are still a problem, the cone should be emptied so that the icing can be stirred until it seems sufficiently smooth. The icing must be free from the aeration which can result when it sits for too long a time without being remixed.

USE THE LEFT HAND TO STEADY THE CONE

Although the right hand (if the decorator is right handed) does most of the work, the left hand is responsible for steadying the cone; indeed, this is an important role which must not be overlooked. The left hand should be held with the palm toward the decorator and with the index and middle fingers extended. These two fingers should lend support either to the decorating cone, or to the heel of the right hand so as to keep it steady and to prevent it from shaking. The left hand should NOT be used to grip the lower portion of the cone, but should merely be used to provide support and unwavering guidance.

Of course the idea of this lesson is not just to restrict the student to practicing his wrist action and his pressure control, it is also to teach the art of creating attractive border designs. These simple border forms can be modified and combined into elaborate designs that will enhance the beauty of the finest cake.

The only limiting factor in the number of handsome or intricate border patterns that can be created is one's own imagination and good taste. It is important for the student to keep in mind that every curve must be graceful so that the pattern flows smoothly, without any abrupt angles or lines that oppose the basic layout.

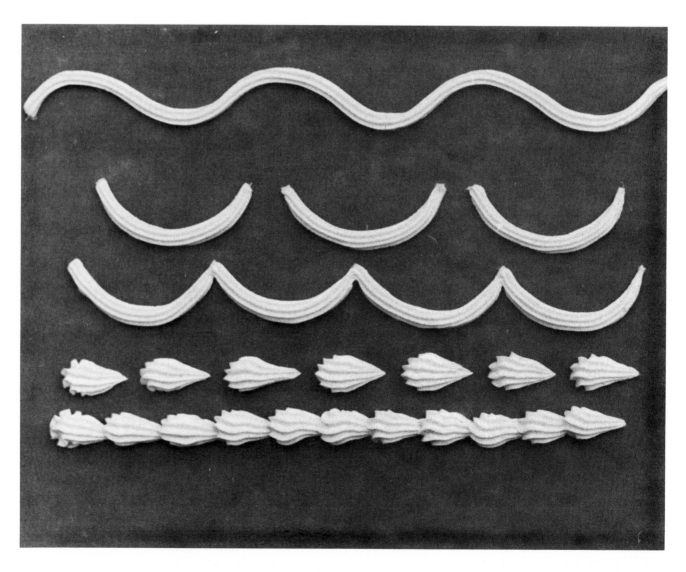

USE PRACTICE BORDERS TO LEARN CONTROL

WAVES

Practice this wavy line. Keep the rise and fall equal each time. Try to confine it between two imaginary boundaries to keep the curves graceful and smooth. Let this action be initiated from the shoulder so that the whole arm can swing freely as it moves in a rhythmical pattern to complete each wavy line. Maintain constant pressure while the decorating cone travels across the practice surface at a smoothly regulated speed and keep the decorating tip in light contact with that surface.

SWAGS

This scalloped edging is made up of individual swags. To get the feel of stopping and starting the motion that is necessary to the correct formation of each segment of the border, practice one swag at a time before attempting to connect them in a series. Use steady, even pressure to form each curve; then cut the pressure to complete one swag before beginning the next. Be sure that all of the segments in the series are uniform. If the lines appear to be ripply, relax the pressure and move the decorating cone with more speed, but don't forget to interrupt the flow of icing at the end of each swag.

SHELLS

The shell border is one of the simplest forms for edging a cake; each shell is like a teardrop. Hold the decorating cone at about a 45 degree angle to the work surface. Push out a bubble of icing, then relax the pressure and stretch the icing to a point. To begin the bubble, hold the decorating tip slightly above the work surface, then let it rise with the increase of pressure; when the pressure is gradually relaxed the tip will descend to the work surface as the shell is pulled to a point. This procedure will require a certain amount of wrist action. As the icing bubble begins to build, slightly turn the wrist clockwise to allow the icing to rise; then let the wrist turn back to its original position at the end of the teardrop's formation. Continue the motion after releasing the pressure, while keeping the tip in contact with the surface, to produce a clean cut-off appearance.

Now connect the shells in a continuous border. Be careful to keep all the shells in exact proportion and in a level line. If the texture that is formed by the star tip appears to be indistinct or to be ruffled, too much pressure is being applied. Reduce the pressure and increase the speed.

"C" CURVES

For the "C" curve and for its upside down counterpart, hold the decorating cone so that it is nearly perpendicular to the work surface, and keep the decorating tip in light contact with that surface. Move the cone in a smooth, perfect arc for the first two-thirds of the "C." Then, while relaxing the pressure, let the icing trail off in a graceful tail. If the decorating tip is not kept in near contact with the surface, it will allow the icing to take short cuts rather than to follow the circular motion of the hand. If it still seems difficult to form a good, smooth arc, practice a series of complete circles to become accustomed to the proper arm movement.

"S" CURVES

Try to execute the "S" curve with absolutely even pressure, then cut the pressure abruptly at the end of the line. Maintain equal-sized circular forms at each end of the "S" and repeat the pattern again, while gradually increasing both speed and accuracy. Keep the decorating cone perpendicular to, and in light contact with, the work surface—just as it was during the execution of the previous exercise.

SHELL VARIATIONS

Try these variations of the shell border. The first is a combination of the shell and the "C" curve. This modified "C" is a smaller arc; however, it is formed with wrist action rather than with the movement of the whole arm. These segments will need to be stretched longer than those in the basic shell border, with each shell overlapping to cover the one before. The second variation is only slightly different from the first. Instead of reversing every other shell, pipe three upward "C" shells, then three reversed shells.

The "daisy" pattern illustrates another use for the basic shell. Each daisy is composed of shells of three different lengths, surrounding a dot which marks the center of the blossom. The tail of each shell points toward, but does not touch, the center dot. Begin with a long shell on each side. Place short shells above and below the dot and finish with medium length shells to fill in the vacant spaces for a total of eight petals. Use these attractive border flowers to form "daisy chains" around the perimeter of a cake. Finish white blossoms with yellow centers, or try different pastel color combinations.

119

120

RIPPLES

Begin a long, straight line of even up-and-down strokes, with the decorating cone held at a 45 degree angle to the work surface. The jiggling motion should be produced from wrist action, not from the movement of the whole arm. Maintain steady pressure, and progress slowly; also, make each line as level as possible. Experiment with lines of different widths to become accustomed to the feel of the motion and the pressure.

RIPPLE VARIATIONS

Try varying the width of the rippled strokes within a single, long line. Begin each segment with short strokes, using light pressure, while holding the decorating tip close to the practice surface; as the length of the strokes increases, so should the pressure, and the star tip should be allowed to rise gradually to accommodate the greater volume of icing. As the segment narrows, shorten the strokes, reduce the pressure, and let the decorating tip descend back to the work surface.

Practice these basic steps until the exercise becomes comfortable and natural. Apply the same method to the scalloped "swag" border. Then experiment with other designs like the "heart" border. Each heart is merely two diagonal shells piped closely together so that they converge at their points. The hearts may be piped in a series, or they may be interrupted at intervals with rippled swags.

OVERPIPED DESIGNS

The continuous "C," modified with overpiping, becomes an ornate and handsome border. Begin with a connected series of "C" curves. These "C" formations are somewhat like the "S" curve—the tail of each "C" swings downward in a short clockwise curve at the end where the next segment will overlap.

The first overpiping is done with gracefully curved lines which intersect the primary "C" formation. Make each intersection smooth by integrating the lines with little pressure, and by taking pains to see that the tail of the overpiped formation follows the same graceful pattern as does the curved line of the original "C."

The textured overpiping is a combination of the modified shell and the ripple. At the beginning, pipe closely overlapping "C" shells to cover most of the curve. Graduate these shells so that they become smaller as they cover the arc; then, change the motion into a rippled line. Follow the curve exactly, and reduce the pressure enough to ease the ripple smoothly into the previously established line of the "C" curve.

STRING WORK AND SUSPENDED SWAGS

Whether dropped in bold swags from a star tip, or dropped in tiny delicate patterns of lace from a small hole cut at the tip of a parchment cone, suspended swags or string work will add an airy, free-flowing touch of charm and beauty to the SIDES of a decorated cake. PLAIN TIPS from parchment cones must be cut carefully, with sharp scissors, so that a clean opening is formed. Any rough places on the cut will cause the icing to hang up or to be malformed, or to come out of the cone in a curl rather than in a nice, smooth, round string.

Prepare the cake or other work surface by dividing its top edge into equal segments of one to two inches. Depending on the diameter of the cake, it will be marked into eight, twelve, or perhaps more sections.

Begin with a dot of firm pressure to secure the string at one of the marks on the edge of the cake. Maintain some pressure and draw the tip outwardly from the surface of the cake while moving it toward the second mark. Do not allow the strand of icing to touch the side of the cake until the bottom of the loop has reached a desirable length. Now touch the tip into the second mark and fasten the string with a dot of firm pressure. Repeat the same pattern to the third mark and continue around the side of the cake. Take care so that each loop drops to just the same depth as the one before, for a uniform appearance. It will probably be necessary to practice several rows of these loops before any uniformity is achieved, but the pressure and speed will soon become automatic.

Variations of the string border are nearly unlimited. Pipe a second or third row of loops above the first row, graduating them so that each row of loops is shallower than the one before, to create a sheer cascade.

For an even lacier effect, make one set of two loops. Then, instead of continuing from the second point to the third point for the next set of double loops, start them midway between the first and second points and extend the strings to midway between the second and third points so that one set of loops overlap the preceding cascade.

Delicate string work patterns may also be artfully applied as inner borders on the tops of cakes. String designs inside a main border of a large sheet cake help to shrink the total area so that smaller, more delicate floral arrangements will adequately fill the space that might otherwise require an awkward, less tasteful composition.

DEVELOP GOOD PRACTICE TECHNIQUES

Throughout the studies of this chapter, strong emphasis has been placed on pressure control, wrist action, and arm movements with which the decorator may not have had previous experience. One should not practice too hard and for so long a time that he might become discouraged. He should put the cone aside, relax, and allow himself time to think about it. Tension builds with one's effort to improve accuracy, and muscles sometimes become too weary to respond for good pressure control and for the necessary smooth motion.

USE SIMPLE BORDER FORMS TO CREATE COMPLEX BORDER DESIGNS

On the following page are several examples of more complex designs that use many of the simpler borders in combination with graceful lines, ripple patterns, and string work. One should always keep in mind the idea that his designs should not be cluttered in appearance and that the border should be integrated into the total decoration of the cake.

CHAPTER IV
Flowers

Basic Rose
Carnation
Chrysanthemum
Pine Cone
Dogwood Blossom
Orchid
Poinsettia
Daffodil

Flowers

There are many beautiful flowers that can be formed with buttercream. This chapter is devoted to some very special blossoms that will, when artistically mastered, be almost the image of nature's most lovely flowers. These flowers will possess such natural formations and contours that one might be tempted to sniff their fragrant bouquet.

The most common difficulties for the student decorator, when he is practicing formation of flowers, are *excessive pressure* and *lack of control in wrist action*. Pressure control and wrist action must be so thoroughly committed to the mind that they become almost involuntary. The importance of pressure control and wrist action have been discussed in previous chapters of this book, and if the student has carefully practiced the exercises leading to this portion of the study, mastering the formation of the various flowers will be faster and easier. If it is difficult for him to coordinate the necessary pressure and motion, the student should return to the chapter on borders and should resume his practice.

When the decorator is able repeatedly to create the flowers without any great effort or concentration, his speed will increase, and the result will be production flower arrangements. The real bonus will be beautiful, natural-appearing roses, carnations, chrysanthemums, orchids, poinsettias, and other flowers that will increase the marketability of his cakes, will encourage repeated sales, and will fulfill the decorator's creative desires. When the artist is truly satisfied with the results of his decorating efforts, the person who receives the cake will almost always be pleased.

One should try to create flowers in colors as nearly like their natural tones and tints as possible. For the decorator to learn the correct proportions and the accurate formation of a blossom, and then to choose a color that is not readily associated with that flower is in poor taste. Such a contradiction should be avoided unless a customer insists (and one occasionally does). In such instances, let this responsibility lie with the person who orders the cake.

It's true that many hybrids of today have varied tones and unusual combinations of color, however, it is a wiser practice to choose the colors more commonly associated with each particular specie for immediate identification.

Although many flowers are not actually variegated, a strip of white or a softer tint of the color selected for the blossom, added to the top inner surface of the cone in line with the fine edge of the tip, creates an illusion of highlight and makes the petal's edge appear to be thinner and more delicate. If the flower is to be a very soft pastel, white icing, delicately blended into the tip of the petal, will provide the satisfactory highlights. In deeper colored blossoms, one should use a softer tint of that same color. The decorator should take great care in blending the two tones to achieve a soft gradation of color, rather than a harsh line where the hues converge.

SELECT THE PROPER TOOLS

If the reader has given close attention to the earlier chapters of this book, he should have assembled all of the equipment necessary to the study and practice of the flowers in this chapter. These tools are designed for special purposes and they are adequate for the most experienced decorator. They require little care, except that it is important that the scissors, skewers, and decorating tips be cleaned after each use, and that the tips should be stored carefully so that they will not be misshapen or damaged.

DECORATING TIPS

Observe the narrow end of the rose tip and note that the slit or opening is wedge-shaped; wide at the base and tapered to a point at the top. Refer to this opening as the "bit," to the wide part of the bit as the "heel," and to the narrow part as the "toe."

The Number 125 rose tip will be adequate for most flowers in this lesson. It is versatile enough that, with controlled pressure, one can form flowers in a wide range of sizes. This saves the time and inconvenience of frequently changing tips. Except for the amount of pressure and the size of the flower, there is no appreciable difference in the make-up of flowers with another sized rose tip. So that the reader will be familiar with these slight differences, he should spend some time practicing with a Number 104 rose tip, and should then be able to make his own choice of tips according to whichever effect he desires to produce.

THE PARCHMENT CONE, FILLING AND BLENDING

The description and method for rolling a parchment cone is thoroughly explained in Chapter I under the heading PARCHMENT PAPER DECORATING CONES. Mastering the skill of rolling the cone is tricky, but it soon becomes a quick and easy task after a bit of experience.

To fill the cone, the decorator should turn it so that the open flap of paper is on the right side, pointed downward. If this is not observed, the flap can sometimes be in the way and may dig into the decorations.

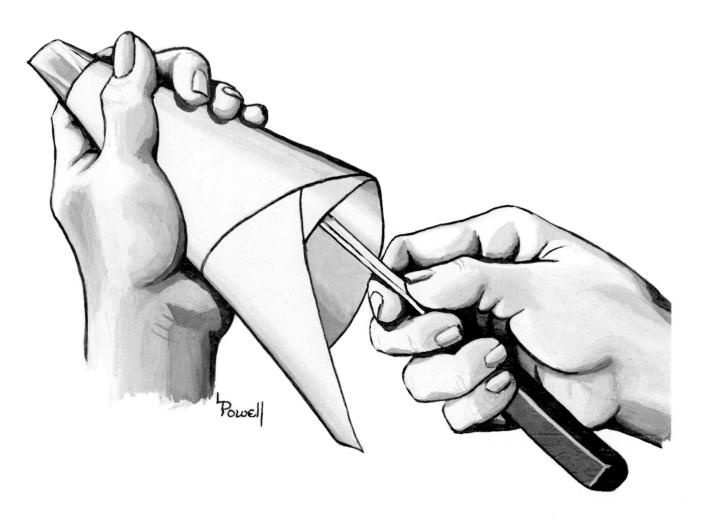

Place the rose tip into position so that the "toe" of the decorating tip is aimed upward. (The toe of the "bit" forms the thin, delicate tip of the flower's petals.) To create a smooth blend of variegated colors within the cone, begin by placing the lighter tone of icing into the upper portion of the cone. This strip of icing should occupy only about 1/4 of the inner surface of the cone. With a small amount of the deeper color on a bowl knife, gently blend it into the lighter-toned icing, taking care not to scrape through the light tone to the inner edge of the decorating cone. If the deeper hue is allowed to penetrate through the lighter tone to the surface of the cone, it will create an unwanted dark streak in the flower petal as the icing is forced out. Finish filling the cone with the deeper color and it is ready for decorating.

DECORATING TIPS CAN BE RESHAPED

If ever the ribbon of icing seems too thick and bulky for proper execution of the flower petals, remove the tip from the cone and slightly close the heel of the bit. Grip the heel with pliers and gently squeeze until it narrows. It may be necessary to reshape the opening of the bit, as it sometimes buckles or closes more than is desirable. Simply insert a narrow scissors or knife blade into the slot and gently pry it back to the proper size and shape. Take care not to mar the edges of the bit, as a rough surface will cause the icing to hang up or even to tear. If this does occur, polish the rough edge with fine emery paper.

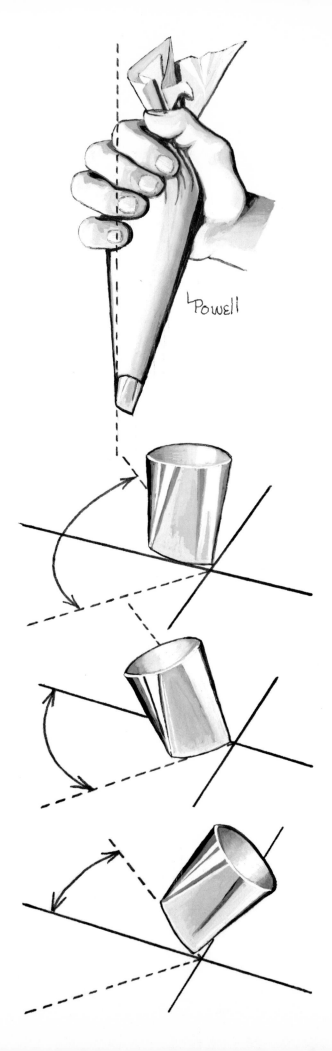

HOW TO HOLD THE DECORATING CONE

The position of the decorating cone, as it is held in the right hand, is of great importance. The cone should not be so over-filled that the end cannot be twisted firmly to form a good seal. Grasp the twisted end tightly in the cradle formed by the thumb and forefinger, in such a manner that the cone and fist form a 90 degree angle with the forearm. Looking from the top of the hand, directly down the cone to the point, the top of the rose tip should be in a straight line with the middle knuckle of the forefinger. A tight grip around the twisted end of the cone should always be maintained. Occasionally it will be necessary to twist the cone more tightly as the icing is spent. The pressure control will depend mostly on the other three fingers, not on the thumb and forefinger.

Positioning the cone in line with the first knuckle of the forefinger in this manner allows adequate arcing of the tip when the proper wrist action is employed. Thus, when bending the hand either to the left or to the right, the tip can be fanned in an arc from a 45 degree angle at the left to a 45 degree angle at the right.

130

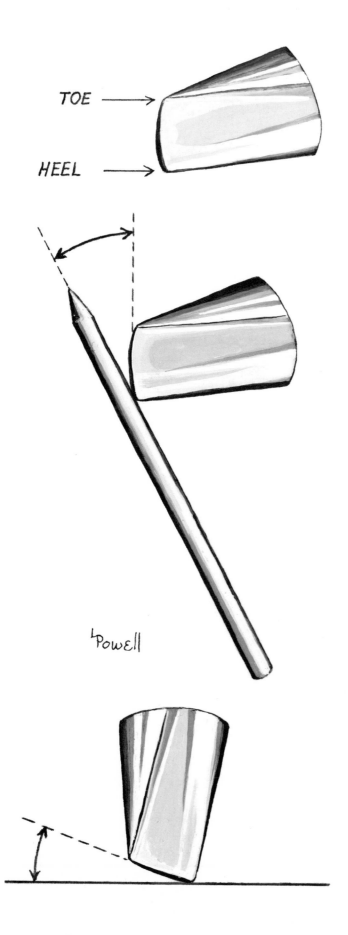

TOE

HEEL

Powell

RELATION OF THE TIP TO THE DECORATING SURFACE

Particular attention must be given to the correct angle of the decorating tip in relation to the surface to which the icing will be applied. Note that from a side view, the "bit" of the rose tip is cut at a slant. This slant, and its relative position to the skewer or to any other decorating surface, will be very important to the formation of the flower petals. In this chapter, reference will frequently be made to the position of the bit, such as: "the bit should be parallel to the skewer," or "the heel of the bit should be in contact with the cake or the work surface," etc., so be aware of this important factor.

If the flower is being piped directly onto the cake, the angle of the bit, as it relates to the work surface, will be determined by wrist action. This precise wrist movement is illustrated and explained in detail on page 168. On the other hand, if the flower is being formed on a wooden skewer or on a plastic straw, the angle of the bit will be affected by how far the top of the skewer (or straw) is tipped back, away from the decorator. Coordination is the key to the expert formation of the flowers in this text; coordination of wrist action, of arm movement and of pressure control with that important element, speed.

WOODEN SKEWERS VERSUS FLOWER NAILS

Many decorators are accustomed to making flowers on a nail; however, there are some advantages to making buttercream blossoms on skewers or on plastic drinking straws. The flower nail has one major drawback. When the decorator forms a blossom on a nail, he is restricted to building a somewhat shallow bud, and the resulting flower usually appears to be flat rather than to be deep and well rounded like its realistic counterpart. By contrast, this illustration shows how flowers which are made on a skewer have shape and depth comparable to a natural blossom. Flower buds wrapped around a skewer can be of greater length and the petals formed about them can be tapered close to the base of the bud and can be fuller in the mid-section, more like a natural blossom.

Occasionally it is appropriate to use the same technique as is employed with the skewer to form blossoms on a plastic drinking straw. Such flowers can be left on their drinking straw stems, and these straws may be inserted into a cake to provide support for the blossom. This procedure is ideal when the decorator finds it necessary to place flowers on the sides of a cake such as one might need to do for a cascading arrangement on a wedding cake.

HOW TO HOLD AND MANIPULATE THE SKEWER

Place the skewer in the left hand (for right-handed people) and position it between the tips of the fingers and the first joint of the thumb. Just spin the skewer toward the thumb-tip—the forefinger and middle finger do most of the work, while the others serve to balance and to guide the skewer.

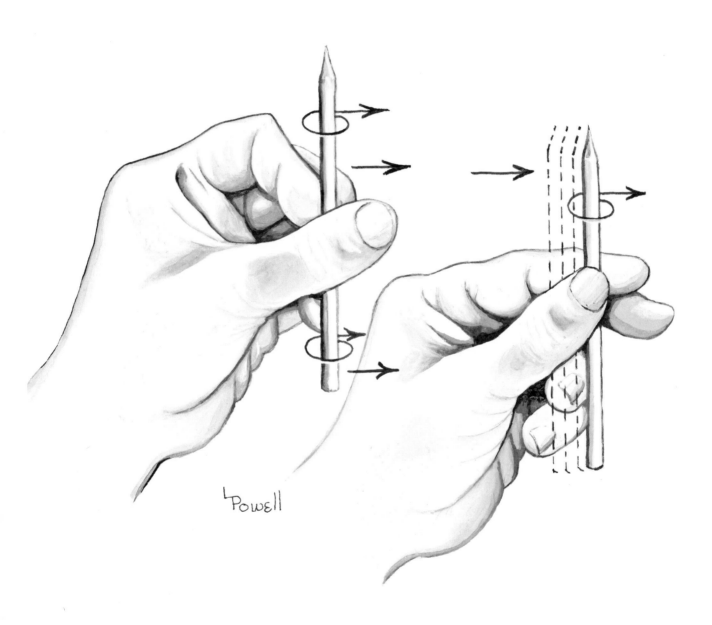

Powell

Once the skewer has been rotated to the tip of the thumb, it must be spun back to the starting position to allow its full rotation on the next twirl. Practice spinning the skewer several times until it seems to be natural and comfortable. It is best to become familiar with this action before trying to form a flower.

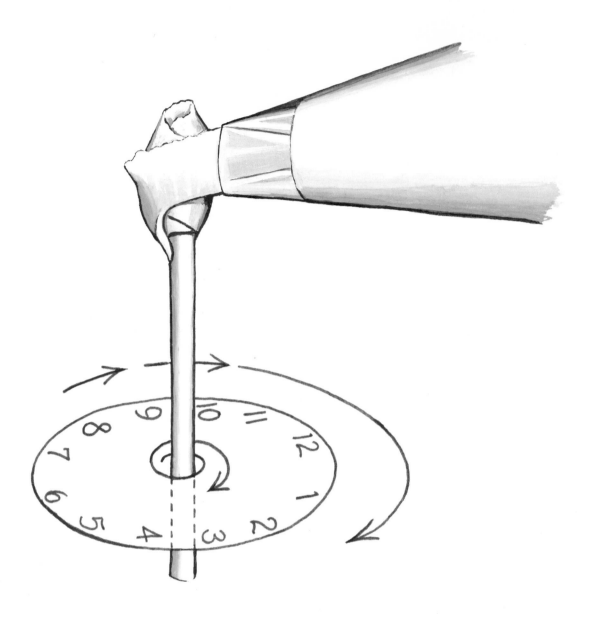

Most people who are experienced in decorating have learned to form their flower petals from right-to-left while rotating the nail or skewer counterclockwise. With that method the decorating tip is always between the flower and the decorator's view. If, instead, the skewer is turned clockwise, and if the petals are formed from left-to-right, one can always see exactly what is taking place as the flower matures to full bloom. Why work in the dark?

HOW TO REMOVE A COMPLETED BLOSSOM FROM THE SKEWER

For the easy removal of any flower from the skewer, slip the scissor blades underneath the blossom, astraddle the skewer. Slowly spin the skewer while simultaneously lifting the flower. Set the blossom on the cake and close the scissors, then use the tip of the skewer to hold the base of the flower in position while pulling the scissors free.

ROSE

This rose is produced in a style unique to this writer. It is formed on a wooden skewer that is operated in a clockwise direction, and its development is basic to that motion and control which is necessary for successfully creating the other flowers in this chapter.

Almost every reader of this book will have previously learned to make roses and shall recognize that this method is unusual; most likely, it will be a hard task for him to change to this style of rose. Well-rooted habits are difficult to break, but it will be necessary to make the change to this style if the student hopes to learn the processes in the development of those more complicated flowers which follow. The pressure control and wrist actions that are involved in all of these blossoms are directly related to this rose.

BASIC WRIST ACTION FOR THE ROSE PETALS

Some of the petals of the rose require the decorating tip to be moved in a simple horseshoe pattern; others, particularly those in the final row, require special wrist action to produce a fan-like flare. The student should find it helpful to practice this method on a flat work surface before applying the icing to the skewer. If one perfects this petal first, and then learns to coordinate the skewer motion with the application of the icing, he should have almost no difficulty creating a full and realistic blossom.

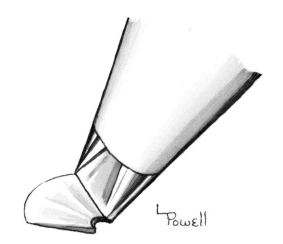

The creation of this fan-shaped petal can best be understood if the reader would compare the sides of the petal with the angles formed by the hands on the face of a clock. The arching motion of the decorating tip should be about the same as that of the large minute hand as it travels from the 10 o'clock to the 2 o'clock position.

Controlled wrist action is extremely important. When holding the decorating cone, be sure that it is in the correct position by checking to see that the toe of the tip is in a direct line with the middle knuckle of the forefinger. Without this alignment, the freedom of wrist movement is hampered.

The hand should bend from the wrist, first to the left to begin the petal, then to the right to complete the motion. The toe of the decorating tip must move in an arc while the heel remains in a nearly stable position.

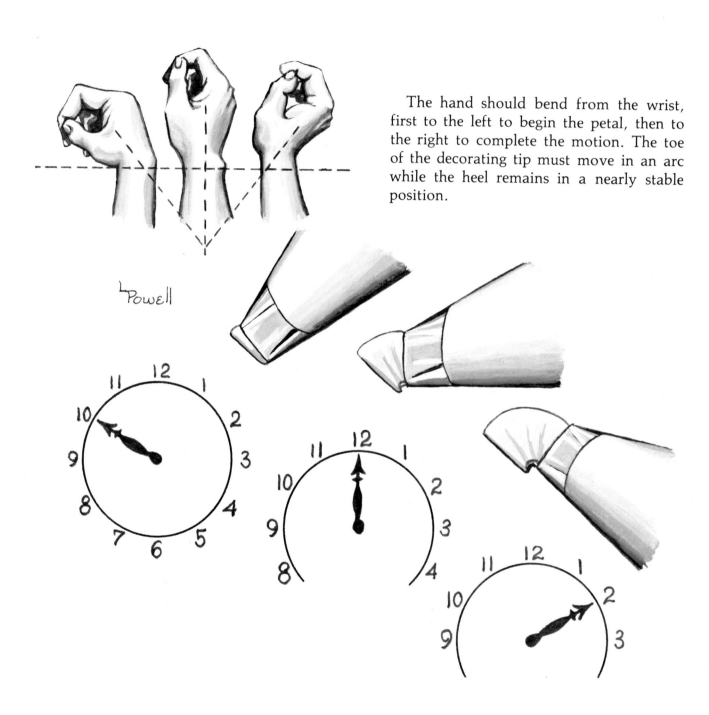

Powell

Fasten the ribbon at the 10 o'clock position and maintain light pressure as the hand and cone turn to 12 o'clock, and continue this motion to complete the stroke at 2 o'clock. Stop the pressure and, while keeping the contact with the icing, slide the tip down toward the base of the petal to sever the ribbon.

136

FORM THE FOUNDATION

The first step in making the rose is to build a foundation or "bud." The right foundation plays a key role in most blossoms. It provides shaping; but more importantly, when properly formed, it will support the flower and prevent it from sliding down the skewer before it is completed. The icing must be *stretched* so that each layer of ribbon is wrapped tightly over the skewer. Take care not to use any more pressure than is necessary. Excessive, uneven pressure will add bulk in unwanted areas and will cause a weak foundation. Decorators who are unaccustomed to making flowers on a skewer usually tend not to turn the skewer fast enough when piping the foundation. Awareness and concentrated practice will soon eliminate any problems in this area.

FORM THE FIRST LAYER

For the first layer of ribbon, the bit should remain parallel to the skewer. Use only enough pressure to fasten the ribbon of icing.

While turning the skewer, stretch the icing ribbon upward to cover the tapered point, then move the decorating tip downward to fasten the band of icing across and to just beyond where it began. At the end of the spin, stop the pressure to cut off the icing. The size of this foundation determines the finished size of the flower.

This single foundation is sufficient for very small blossoms. Roses of medium size may also be formed over such a foundation.

To create larger blossoms, pipe additional ribbons of icing over the primary foundation, only begin each one lower on the skewer, gradually raising the ribbon until it completely covers over the first layer of foundation. This band should finish on a downward stroke near its origin.

By beginning each successive band low and wrapping it completely over the initial layer of foundation, a smooth football-shaped form results. This will achieve the bulk necessary for the proper fullness of the blossom.

FORM THE FIRST ROW OF PETALS

The first row will contain three narrow petals. Turn the skewer slowly for the petals and use *very light* pressure.

FIRST PETAL

Begin low on the bud to secure the ribbon, then move the tip upward abruptly to extend the petal above the height of the bud while gradually twirling the skewer. Maintain a steady but light pressure and proceed with the downward stroke to complete the first petal near the base of the bud.

SECOND PETAL

The skewer should have revolved only a little more than a half-turn for the first petal. Back the skewer so that the second petal begins to overlap the first about midway. Repeat the same motion as for the first petal.

THIRD PETAL

Lap the third petal over the second in the same fashion and this row of petals will be complete.

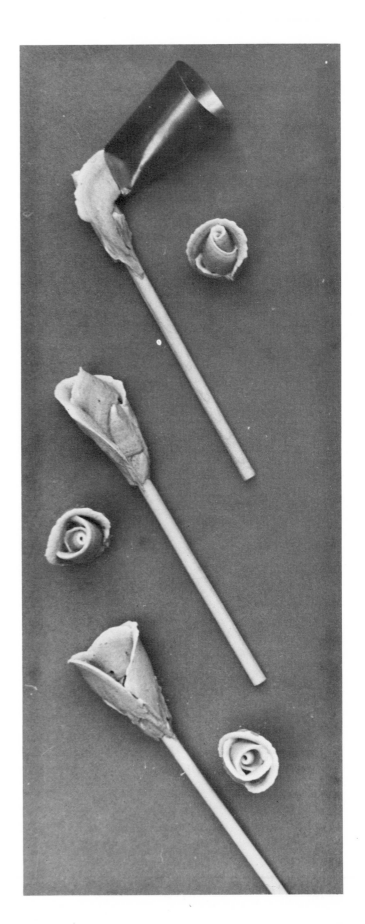

NO SET NUMBER OF PETALS

There should be no set rule for numbers of petals for roses and similarly complex blossoms. The main objective always should be to create the most natural-appearing flowers possible. The step-by-step formations as per the instructions in this chapter are merely guide lines and may be varied according to the desire of the decorator. In fact, random numbers of petals serve to distinguish one flower from the next, and help to increase interest and eye-appeal. One of the most important things for the decorator to remember is that he should strive to keep the petals narrow, not wider than one and one-half times the length of the bit.

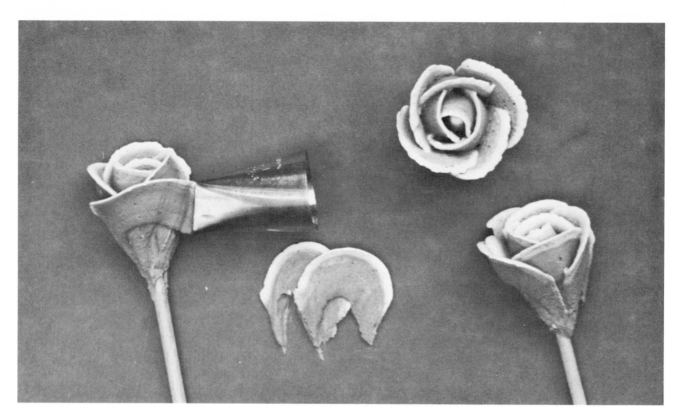

FORM THE SECOND ROW OF PETALS

To this point, the bit and the skewer should have remained quite parallel. For the second row, the toe of the bit should be out slightly away from the previous row of petals. Rather than to tip the decorating cone to an uncomfortable position, allow the skewer to angle backward and to the left, away from the decorating cone. Take care to keep the heel of the bit in contact with the icing so that the new petals are fastened firmly to the flower.

Starting each petal at the base of, or slightly below, the foundation will help to build necessary support for the completed blossom.

In the second row, each petal should reach a height just below the top of the first row of petals. Overlap enough of each new petal so that it does not fasten directly in line with any of the petals in the previous row. Each layer of petals should be staggered for a more natural appearance. Of course each petal in this row should overlap the one before in just the same manner as did those in the first row.

FORM THE FINAL ROW OF PETALS

The final row, whether it is the second, third, or fourth layer, should be made with fan-shaped petals. On larger roses the decorator may need to employ some of this wrist action on petals before the final row. It should be noted here that the fullness which is created by this action causes the petals to flare outward at the top. Experience and practice will show the decorator when and where to use this technique for the most desirable results.

The application of these petals to the blossom is exactly the same as for the previous rows of petals. Remember to start at the base of the blossom and to overlap each petal the same as before.

If this exercise remains difficult after several tries, set the skewer aside and return to practicing this petal on a flat surface. This way one concentrates solely on the action of the cone, without concern about coordinating it with the additional motion of the skewer. Remember to use only enough pressure to form a smooth, unbroken petal. Too much pressure will make the petal wrinkled and heavy, and to appear to be malformed. When well-shaped petals can be formed repeatedly without concentration on the motion, resume practicing the complete flower on a skewer. After the student is able to complete this style rose to his satisfaction, he should practice forming blossoms of various sizes. For this it may be necessary to return to the instructions on how to form the foundation.

FORM ROSE BUDS ON THE CAKE

Rose buds can be formed directly on the cake. These can range in form from closed, new buds, to open, nearly full blossoms. Before trying this exercise, it will be helpful if the student tries to imagine a real flower as it unfolds from a new bud to various stages of bloom. The new bud is a tightly massed cluster of petals. In the first stage of its evolution, the outer row of petals pulls away from the bud. As they continue to flare, the next row of petals begins to open, and so the process goes on until just a small cluster remains at the center of the blossom.

To form the "new bud," fasten the ribbon of icing on the work surface and, maintaining slight pressure, move the tip forward a distance comparable to about half the length of the bit. At the top of the motion, shift slightly to the right and move the tip back down, then left to the original starting position. Continuing with the same pressure, repeat the motion; except this time, the upward stroke should be shorter and the ribbon should be severed with the downward motion.

Progressive phases of blooming can be simulated with the addition of extra petals to the new bud. The first phase is a new bud with two fan-shaped petals on either side. Start with a new bud and, beginning on its left, pipe a fan-shaped petal that extends from the work surface to beyond the center of the bud. The second petal should start at the right side of the bud and fan to the left so that its formation is exactly reversed from the first petal. The fuller bud in the next phase begins with two fan-shaped petals piped on the cake first, then a new bud with petals on each side. One more petal fanned across the flower, at the position where the last two petals intersect, will complete this phase.

Practice these variatons, always keeping the heel of the tip in close proximity to the base of the bud so that the bottom of the flower is narrowed almost to a point.

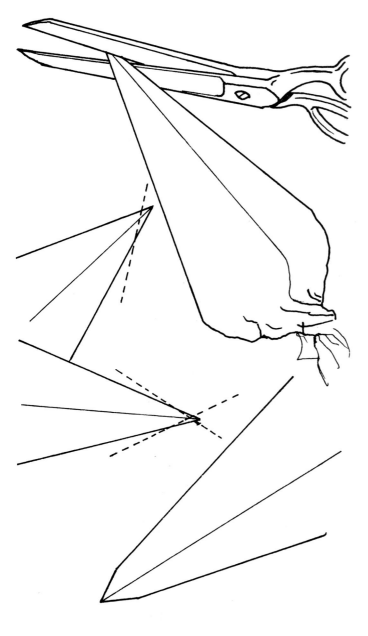

ROSE FOLIAGE

Although special tips are available for making assorted sizes of leaves, this decorator prefers to make leaves with parchment cones that are cut especially for this purpose. After filling a cone with icing, turn it so that the seam is centered on the top. Flatten the point and use scissors to carefully cut it on an angle.

Rotate the cone a half-turn and cut the other side to a matching angle.

Notice that this cone is cut to a sharp point. If the point is too blunt, the resulting leaves will be heavy and misshapen.

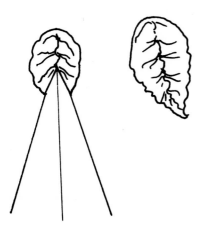

Squeeze out some icing to test the shape, and check to see that both halves of the grooved ribbon of icing are equal. If one side appears to be narrower than the other, reflatten the cone and trim just enough off that edge to correct the defect.

143

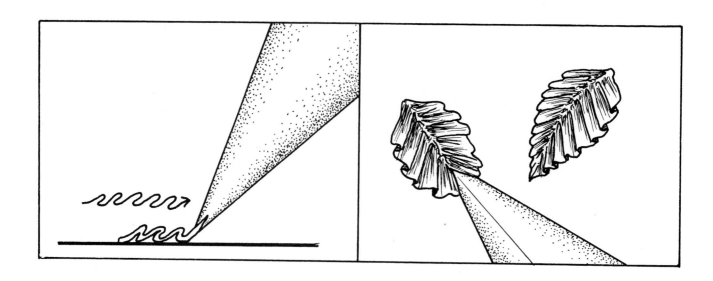

FORM THE LEAVES

Hold the cone at about a 45 degree angle, with the point touching the work surface. Begin applying pressure, then increase it so that the leaf widens as the cone is pulled away from the starting place. Gradually raise the tip from the surface and, when the length of the leaf seems to be in proper proportion to its width, relax the pressure until the leaf stretches to a point. Jiggling the cone in and out or sideways as the leaves are formed will produce a pattern similar to the texture of a real rose leaf.

ARRANGE THE STEMS AND LEAVES

To make a stem cone, flatten the point of a small parchment cone, and snip just enough off the point to create a small hole about the size of a pencil lead. With a normal amount of pressure, this should create a fine string that doesn't curl when piped over the cake. Draw out the stems to the proper design, add the flowers and buds, and then arrange the leaves. Remember to first pipe the leaves nearest the main grouping of blossoms, so that each aims away from the center of interest. Then pipe the remainder of the leaves so that they seem to emanate from stems around the individual buds.

144

145

CARNATION

Carnations are not at all foreign to most cake decorators. They have been used to adorn many special-occasion cakes, but have almost always been formed directly on the cake's surface. The carnation in this book is the author's own creation, and is unusual because it is fashioned on a skewer with a Number 125 rose tip and has the shape and fullness of a natural blossom. The colors of carnations range from white to bright red, and the hues of this spectrum include tones of pink and pastel tints of yellow, orange, and violet.

The intricate network of foliage for this flower must be piped on the cake before the decorator arranges the blossoms. These leaves are slender and must be free to curve and curl gracefully behind the flowers. Free movement of the decorating cone would be hampered if the decorator should attempt to arrange the leaves after the carnations have been placed on the cake.

Since this style of carnation is produced on a skewer, it is very adaptable for use on wedding cakes; often the bride has had to settle for roses. At best, she could hope to have the roses made to match those colors which she had selected for the bouquets and dresses. This chapter provides a decorator with the background to create many blossoms for wedding and all-occasion cakes that will not only match the color theme but that will be in harmony in every way with the bouquets furnished by the florist.

The method for forming the carnation is not so different from that procedure which was employed in making the rose, however, it requires a tremendous amount of concentration in combination with a special emphasis on control of the decorating cone. The ruffled petals of the carnation will tax the most skillful decorator's ability to coordinate motion and controlled pressure. Before the finished blossom is lifted from the skewer, the outer edge of each petal must be clipped with sharp scissors. This step makes the buttercream carnation an almost exact duplicate of its counterpart in nature's wondrous garden.

Carnations must be made from stiff buttercream. For best results, the icing should be as firm as can be easily handled. A really firm buttercream will produce realistic petals with a greatly defined ruffle and a slightly broken edge that will require little clipping with the scissors.

These petals will be about the height of two lengths of the decorating bit; their width should never exceed one length of the bit, and generally should be narrower (half-an-inch or less).

BASIC WRIST ACTION FOR THE CARNATION PETAL

Where the smooth fan-shaped petals of the rose have a tendency to be rounded on the tip, the carnation's ruffled petals should be more square. The effect is achieved by short up-and-down strokes; this action should be initiated at the wrist, rather than from the movement of the whole arm. Movement from just the wrist allows more perfect control. Imagine that the motion required for this ruffling effect is similar to the action a decorator would employ if he held a cone of icing above a saw blade and then rapidly moved the decorating tip to trace the outline of a series of the saw's teeth.

Since the jiggling motion for this petal requires the use of muscles in the wrist that have not previously been trained, it would be advisable for the student to practice a series of long ribbons employing this technique. Unaccustomed to this action, the wrist at first may seem stiff. Repeated practice will gradually make this an effortless, natural movement.

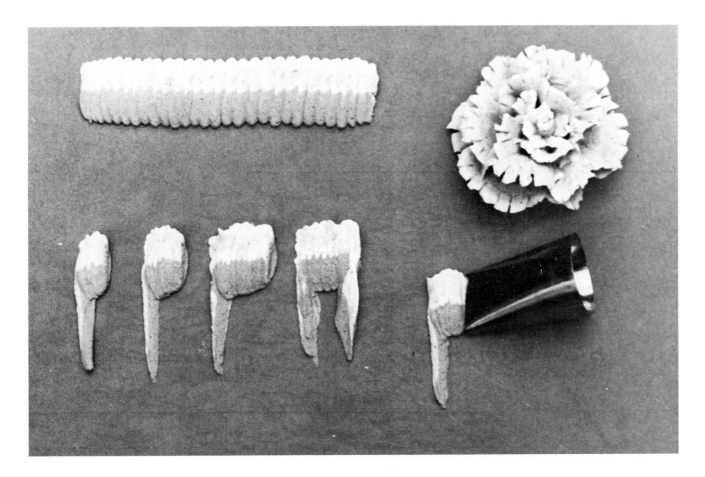

It would be easier if the student would first practice this petal on a flat surface. Start with only sufficient pressure to securely fasten the ribbon of icing, then move the cone straight upward, but use only a little pressure so that the icing is stretched until it reaches the appropriate height for that petal. Increase the pressure enough to keep the icing flowing as the decorating tip follows its saw-tooth pattern to complete the adequate width. Gently press the toe of the bit into contact with the work surface by slightly turning the wrist clockwise, and draw the tip straight downward to finish the petal with a clean cut.

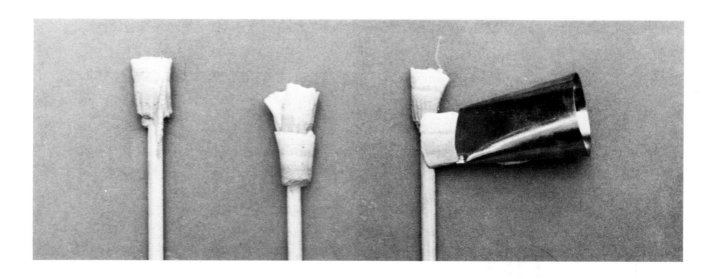

FORM THE FOUNDATION

The foundation is like the petal on the previous page that was practiced on a flat surface. It should be ruffled tightly around the tapered end of the skewer, with its formation built high enough to completely cover the point. A smooth ribbon should then be wrapped firmly about the base of this structure to complete the foundation. This is highly important for support, because this blossom's ruffled petals are much heavier than those that make up the rose. As this blossom takes on additional layers of petals, similar ribbon "supports" must be added to help to carry the increased weight.

From this point on, there is one significant difference between the structure of the rose and that of the carnation. The rose was formed with overlapping petals, BUT THE CARNATION IS MADE WITH ONE PETAL ADJACENT TO THE OTHER. In most instances the sides of these adjacent petals will not touch each other.

FORM THE FIRST ROW OF PETALS

Beginners have a tendency to make the petals for this flower too short and too wide. The student should recognize that his inclination to form disproportionate petals and to use too much pressure will be the greatest difficulties for him to overcome. These problems will be greatly minimized if the reader has practiced the exercises in the earlier pages of this lesson.

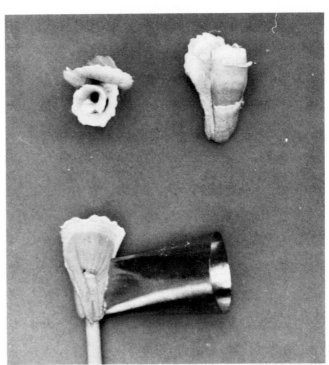

The first row is formed from three narrow petals. Each petal should begin low on the ribbon support and should be stretched to such a height that its tip extends above the top of the foundation. Finish the petal by relaxing the pressure while drawing the decorating tip down to the same level at which the petal was begun.

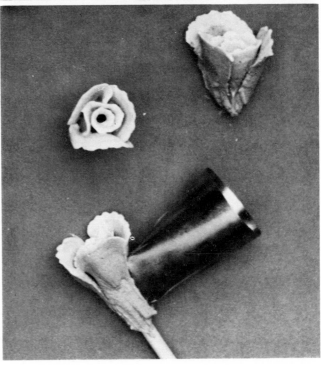

When completed, the petals should cling closely to the foundation. If, on the final downward stroke, the edges of the petals tend to flap outward instead of to wrap tightly against the foundation, it may be difficult to form successive rows of petals. To avoid this unwanted flap on the final stroke, allow the toe of the decorating tip to arc slightly clockwise toward the foundation as it is drawn downward. With this action, the heel of the decorating tip must remain in contact with the previous formation.

149

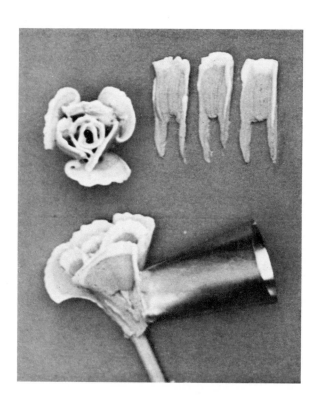

FORM THE SECOND ROW OF PETALS

This row should consist of three narrow petals; narrow enough so that they are not touching each other. Each petal should begin low on the skewer, then it should rise to a peak that is nearly the height of the petals in the first grouping. Pipe each one at a position coinciding with the separation between two petals in the previous row. This placement will help to insure a more natural blossom so that, when the flower is viewed from above, the petals will be staggered instead of being stacked with one directly in a line below the other.

Prepare for the next row by adding a ribbon of icing over the lower portion of this layer of petals to increase the support. The carnation is very open and lacy; in the buttercream flower this openness is achieved by the addition of the "support-ribbon" and by the maintenance of good separation between the petals.

FORM THE FINAL ROWS OF PETALS

For this step, the skewer should be tilted at an angle back from the decorating tip so that these petals commence to flare away from the more compact center of the flower. These rows should contain two sets of three well-separated, narrow petals. Form three petals, then tilt the skewer farther backward and add another set of three petals. When adding the final rows, begin each petal beside the skewer by holding the bit along the "right" side of the shaft. This will help to make the narrow petals stand outward so as to produce the openness that is important to the realistic formation of this carnation.

150

FORM THE FILLER PETALS

Only larger carnations will require these "filler" petals. Use these, as their name implies, to fill out the blossom. Look down upon the top of the flower to see where extra petals might be added to the outside of the blossom to perfect its shape, then make any additions that seem desirable.

COMPLETE THE CARNATION

Before removing the flower from the skewer, carefully clip each petal in two or three places. Hold the skewer so that the top of the carnation is visible. Use very sharp, fine-pointed scissors; dip them into hot water and barely cut into the edge of each petal. Clip one petal, turn the flower, clip the next one, and so on. If the scissors begin to pull the icing instead of to leave a clean cut, wipe them on a cloth and dip them into the hot water again. Use the scissors to lift the flower from the skewer and to position it over the foliage arrangement on the cake.

The number of layers of petals determines the finished size of the carnation. For smaller blossoms, use fewer rows, and allow the petals to flare away sooner from the center mass. Larger flowers will require extra layers of support to precede and to support the additional rows of petals.

151

CARNATION BUD

Carnation buds follow the same procedure as was recommended for the construction of the rose buds, except that the cone should be jiggled to ruffle the top of each petal. Although it is not absolutely necessary, the petals of the bud can be clipped. This is time consuming and doesn't lend that much more realism to a bouquet of carnations.

CARNATION FOLIAGE

The foliage for carnations is composed of slender, curving leaves drawn on the cake in a pattern that expresses the shape of the floral arrangement. These leaves are made with lightly greyed, green icing, variegated with a small amount of blue-green.

Cut the opening in the parchment cone so that it is about half the size of the rose leaf, and not quite so sharply pointed.

Use the leaf cone to draw out the shape of the bouquet, much as one would pipe stems for an arrangement of roses. Then fill in the open area with gracefully curving leaves so that they emanate from the center of interest. The "center of interest" was discussed in Chapter II, and is that place in the arrangement around which the main blossoms are situated. Remember that for best composition, this point should not be in the exact middle of the stem or of the leaf pattern.

152

CHRYSANTHEMUM

In reality these flowers are abundant in many shapes and sizes. Some are clusters of spiney tentacles, others are like daisies; also, their configurations include radiant sunbursts and compact pompons. This text will deal only with the pompon chrysanthemum. Since it is the desire of the author to stimulate and to challenge the imagination of each reader, it is his recommendation that the student should make every effort to explore the other varieties. Once the skills that are needed to create the flowers in this chapter are achieved, they can be applied to the formation of many other blossoms. The trick lies in the decorator's ability to analyze a flower, by examining the structure of the blossom and the shape of each of its petals, and in his use of imagination and skill to recreate the likeness of that flower in icing. This was the basis for the origination of the unique styles of carnations, poinsettias and pine cones in this chapter. Each started from this author's desire to create the most possible realism and this required a break away from previous theories and practices.

Chrysanthemums range in color from fiery autumn hues to elegant lavenders, pinks, and purples, therefore appealing either to masculine or feminine tastes. They offer a pleasant contrast to the much overused rose for wedding cakes and for the decorations of other special occasion cakes. Obviously the chrysanthemum should not be overlooked because of its extreme versatility. It has its exceptions though, as it is seasonal and its general use is limited primarily to the fall of the year.

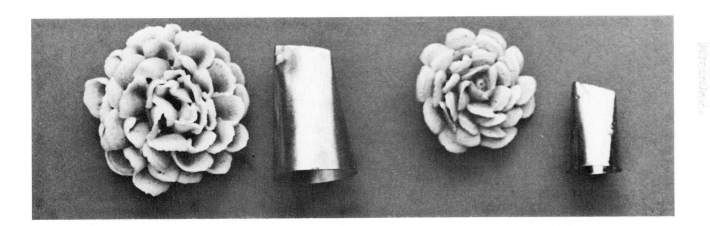

USE THE CORRECT DECORATING TIP FOR PRACTICE

Begin practice on the chrysanthemum with a Number 104 rose tip. This tip will help to minimize the inevitable pressure control problems with this flower. It is particularly difficult to learn to make this blossom with a Number 125 rose tip in the beginning because its greater size allows the icing to flow so easily through the bit. However, once it is mastered with the smaller rose tip, it would be wise to adapt this skill to the larger tip because of its capability to form a greater variety of more-natural blossom sizes.

LEARN THE METHOD

The method for creating this blossom could most nearly be described as legerdemain. The decorator's hand has to move rapidly while his mind must think in terms of not just one petal, but of a complete row at a time. Each petal in the series is shaped like a long, slender teardrop that is almost "paper" thin. Keen control of the pressure must be exercised, and each set of petals must be produced with utmost coordination in a pattern that requires continuous momentum.

Practice individual petals on a flat work surface, enough to get the feeling for the correct shaping. The enlarged examples in the following illustration show the correct shape of a completed petal, and they demonstrate how, on the downward stroke, the decorating tip should arc just before the pressure is cut to sever the decorating ribbon of icing.

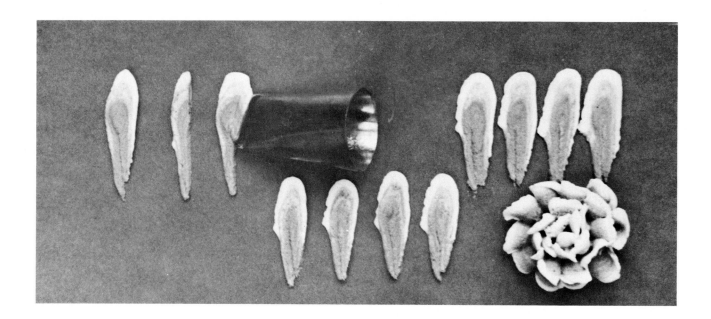

FORM THE BLOSSOM ON A SKEWER

First the ribbon of icing is fastened to the skewer; then, the decorating tip is moved upward. On this quick, elevating stroke, the pressure must swell, and should reach its peak as the toe of the tip is arced clockwise to complete the fan shape at the top of the petal. This is the climax of the pressure, but not of the motion or of the speed. The toe of the decorating bit must immediately be tipped forward toward the skewer, then drawn straight downward to where the petal began.

Unlike that method which was used for the previous flowers in this chapter, the skewer's motion must be uninterrupted during the formation of each petal, then should be moved to allow for the next one to be piped right beside the one before. Chrysanthemum petals, like those of the carnation, do not overlap.

154

FOUNDATION BUD IS NOT NECESSARY

It doesn't seem to make a great difference if one begins with or without a foundation for this blossom. If the flower tends to slide down the skewer, even though each row of petals is begun well below the one before, a tiny bud wrapped tightly over the point of the skewer may be necessary.

The first row should consist of three or four petals. The bit of the decorating tip should be parallel to the skewer for this row, then the skewer should be angled slightly away from the decorating cone for the next set of petals. With the addition of each row, the skewer should be tipped back more and more, to cause the petals to be properly flared. Each row of petals should be started lower on the skewer than the previous row. On the final rows, the decorating tip should begin the upward stroke beside, and directly to the right of, the skewer shaft. In this step, the petal will actually begin from the bottom of the blossom, rather than from the front side of its base; this is necessary in order to give the long, lower petals the support that they need.

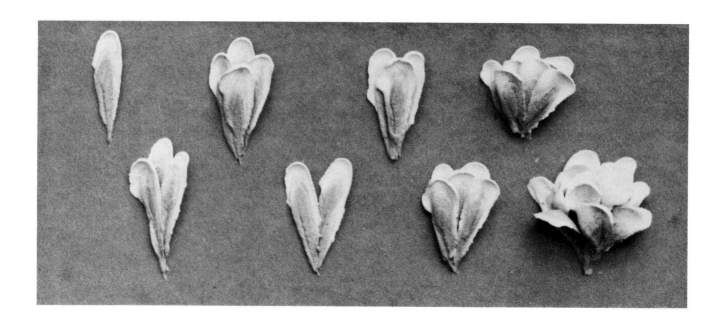

CHRYSANTHEMUM BUD

Form buds for this flower by piping a cluster of chrysanthemum petals on the cake. Take into account the flare of the blossom when making partially opened buds, and angle the decorating tip accordingly.

After practicing all the phases of this flower and becoming thoroughly familiar with its proper formation, try making the chrysanthemum with a Number 125 rose tip. Pressure control will be even more critical, but this is an excellent exercise for training one's fingers to respond with precise timing.

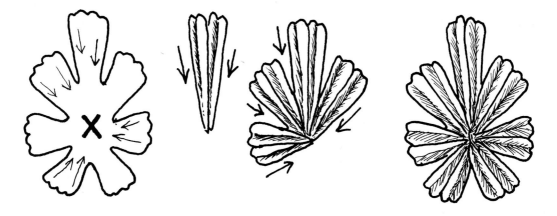

CHRYSANTHEMUM FOLIAGE

A cone cut to form a leaf tip just smaller than the one for rose leaves will be adequate. The shape of the chrysanthemum leaf resembles that of an oak leaf.

Trace over the ink outline of the leaf with a pencil. Make three or four outlines on tracing paper and secure it to the practice surface with dabs of icing. This will serve as a pattern until the student is accustomed to the symmetrical formation of this leaf.

156

The decorating cone should be positioned perpendicularly to the work surface so that the icing is always *pulled* from the tip. Begin at the X at the center of the pattern and move to the top of the leaf and back down to the X. Make the three left fingers of the leaf the same way, then shift to the fingers on the right side of the leaf, noting the length of each appendage. Their different lengths and positions should remain the same in all such leaves, so that the overall pattern is more egg-shaped than round.

Lay out the stems for the bouquet and select a position for the center of interest, then aim each leaf away from that place.

Pipe bubbles of icing on the foliage arrangement to mark the positions for the full blossoms. These bubbles will support the blossoms, allowing them to tip at an angle away from the center of attention. Position the blossoms, then add buds in various phases of bloom.

PINE CONE

The pine family is made up mostly of evergreens with needle foliage and they bear woody blossom-like cones. Beside the true pine, this family includes firs, hemlocks, spruces, etc., each with its separate identity. Some have long needles which fan from a central point. Others bear short needles arrayed about the full length of their stems. This pine cone can be used with either style foliage or may be set into an arrangement of holly or poinsettias to add to the holiday decorations. When used strictly with pine boughs these realistic cones do not necessarily have to be limited to the Christmas season, as they are a fine substitute for floral arrangements for men, especially if the recipient's work or sports activities lend to this theme.

The method for making pine cones is almost exactly the same as for the chrysanthemum. The major difference is that the pine cone is made on a plastic drinking straw (the slender cocktail straw works best). Cut the eight-inch straw in half to make the proper lengths for two pine cones.

Each segment of the pine cone is like the chrysanthemum petal. The pine cone segments should not flare out as much as the outer rows of petals on the flower; therefore, each succeeding row should start even lower on the straw. This will help to add length to the pine cone and at the same time will minimize the bulk.

The pine cone should be built row-by-row until it covers about two-thirds of the length of the straw. The remaining length of the straw will act as a stem to be inserted into the cake to support the pine cone.

To insert the finished pine cone into the cake, move it to the proper location and gently grasp the straw with scissors just below its base, taking special precaution not to squeeze the straw. If the straw is squeezed too tightly, the straw will collapse and will cause the pine cone to tumble onto the cake. The scissors should only hold the straw firmly enough to guide it into final position.

PINE CONE BUD

Pine cones, if considered to be blossoms, could have smaller pine cones piped on the cake in the same manner as the buds about the full blossoms in a floral arrangement. Shape them like small pine cones, using that same technique which was suggested for the formation of chrysanthemum buds, and aim each one away from the center of interest.

158

PINE FOLIAGE

Begin the pine foliage with stems, but keep them in straight lines of differing lengths. The stem should radiate from a dot which marks the center of interest.

The pine needles will line both sides of the stem and are produced from a small hole in a parchment cone. Cut this hole slightly larger than the opening for a stem tip. Make the needles with inch-long back-and-forth strokes, diagonal to the stem so that they also angle away from the center of interest.

Each bough has "spur" stems that protrude to either side. Spurs at either side intersect the main stem at the same place. Those near the top of the stem are shortest; the spurs grow a little longer as they near the base of the bough. It even is acceptable for some of these longer secondary branches to have spurs of their own.

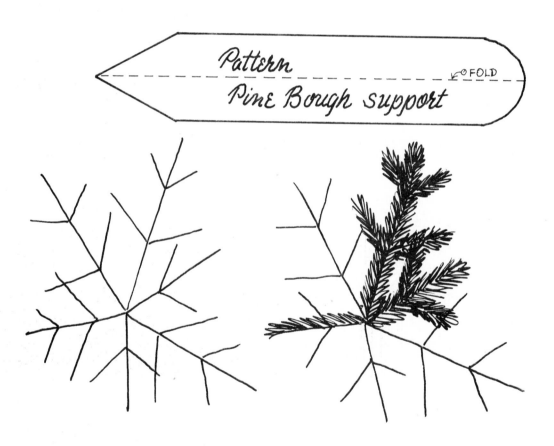

Pine boughs piped over cardbord supports can, when inserted into a cake, add dramatic depth to the arrangement. Trace this pattern, fold it on the dotted line, and use it as a guide to cut supports from folded pieces of firm cardboard. Be certain to insert at least one-third of this support into the cake, otherwise the weight of the icing branch will cause it to tear the cake and will allow the bough to collapse. These supports should be inserted after the stem pattern is drawn on the cake and should be used as an extension of some of the longer stems. Avoid placing them too near the center of the arrangement; there must be sufficient space to allow for the penetration of the pine cone straws.

160

DOGWOOD BLOSSOM

Perhaps this flowering tree, common to the Pacific Northwest and to some New England localities, will not be familiar to some students. Its blossoms are usually off-white, but some of the ornamental varieties are pink. When made in cream-colored icing, with their centers formed of a mixture of tan, green and yellow curls, their simple lines make them ideal flowers for a man's cake. Dogwood blossoms exemplify the man's world—the out-of-doors, the woods where he hunts or fishes.

Making this flower will be a new experience from the earlier flowers in this chapter, as it is piped over an icing foundation on the cake. It has four heart-shaped petals, each narrow at the base, with a double fan at the top. Use of a Number 125 rose tip will make this blossom nearly life-sized.

TRACE AN OUTLINE

Place a piece of tracing paper over the drawing of the single petal and trace an outline to use as a practice guide to learn the positions of the decorating tip.

Do not use any pressure or squeeze out any icing for this exercise. Position the decorating cone over the traced outline of the petal and practice following the positions of the decorating tip just as they are illustrated in the accompanying drawing. Be certain to hold the decorating cone properly so that the toe of the tip is in line with the middle knuckle of the forefinger. Begin at the base of the outline, holding the parchment cone at a 90 degree angle to the work surface. Move in an upward stroke, while gradually changing the arc of the metal tip so that it imitates the positions in the illustration. The heel of the bit should ride just slightly to the right of the center-vein line until about the middle of the upward stroke, then right on the center for the remainder of the petal. This will keep the thin ribbon of icing from drooping as the petal is piped onto the foundation. The double fan shape at the top of the petal is formed by a short downward movement at the center, then the tip must rise again to the previous level before finally making the downward stroke to complete the right half.

At the start of the upward stroke, as this petal is begun, the toe of the metal tip should be aimed just to the left of "12 o'clock." It will gradually arc to about "10 o'clock" at the widest place, then will swing back to "11 o'clock" at the top of the first fan. As the tip moves downward it should straighten to "12 o'clock" to complete the first side of the petal. The tip must then move forward, and turn slightly to the right to begin the second fan. Arc the bit toward "2 o'clock" on the downward stroke to finish the petal.

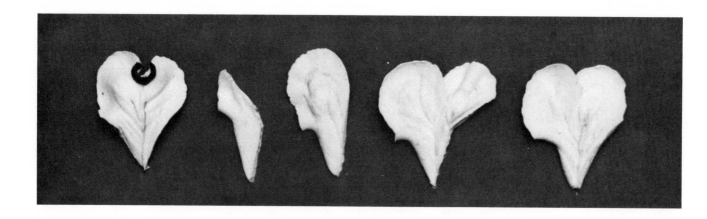

Now practice making the petal with icing. At first it may help to work within one of the outlines on the paper. Beginning at the base of the petal, use just enough pressure to make a thin ribbon of icing as the tip arcs to "10 o'clock." Lightly increase the pressure to form the first fan. Relax the pressure at the center of the petal before starting the next fan. When the second fan is completed, begin relaxing the pressure and actually stretch the ribbon of icing to finish the petal.

After becoming familiar with the pressure control and wrist action to the degree that a petal can be piped with competent accuracy, try making one on a foundation. The foundation is merely a bubble of icing. To learn the right size for this formation, practice within one of the outlines. Simply hold the cone so that it is perpendicular to the paper, squeeze out a bubble, and allow the cone to rise as the bubble grows. This bubble should begin just below the notch between the fans. When the bubble is about a quarter-inch deep, pull the tip down toward the base of the petal; gradually relax the pressure to form a teardrop bubble.

When piping the petal over the foundation, keep the heel of the bit in contact with the icing bubble at all times. If the petal seems droopy, try increasing the speed. If that doesn't help enough, decrease pressure on the next try.

With this and the succeeding flowers that are formed on foundations, make the foundation and petal all in a continuous motion. Do not separate the decorating tip from the foundation before continuing the motion that forms the petal. This will require very accurate pressure control, and will help to eliminate ragged flaws caused from stops and starts between the two forms.

164

Assembly of four petals to form a single blossom will be facilitated by marking the position for the center of the flower with a small dot of icing. Keep a small margin between this dot and the base of each petal to assure a more open, natural assemblage. The center cluster of stamens will connect and integrate the formation.

The center of the flower is like little pods or curls. Prepare a small parchment cone with a narrow strip of brown on one side and green on the opposite; then fill the remaining space with yellow, or yellow and white. Cut the tip of the cone to a very small opening so that the icing comes out in controlled curls when great pressure is applied as the tip is held about a quarter-inch from the work surface. Move the tip of the cone in a small circular pattern to form a round cluster of curls to simulate the little mound of stamens in a real dogwood. Use this same cone to overpipe the tip of each petal where the two fans meet.

DOGWOOD BUD

Buds for this blossom can be like the rose bud. As these flowers mature, the petals drop away, leaving just the seed pod in the center, so this stage can also be represented in the arrangement. Just shape it like the little curled mound at the center of the flower.

DOGWOOD FOLIAGE

The woody stems of the dogwood are brownish green. With this flower, like the procedure for the chrysanthemum and carnation, the foliage will have to be placed on the cake first.

The leaves for this flower are almost as complex as the petals. Don't be discouraged though, as they are quite simple, once mastered, and can be positioned on the cake almost as quickly as rose leaves.

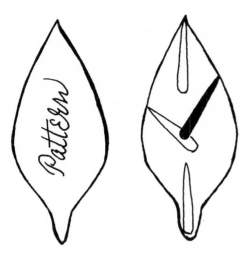 

Trace an outline of the leaf on paper and practice the angles of the decorating tip as they are indicated in the illustration. Then practice this exercise several times with buttercream on a flat surface before attempting the following steps. Now the leaf should be formed on a foundation to give it a more life-like appearance. These foundations give more depth to arrangements, allowing highlights and shadows to form on the background, creating an illusion of a third dimension.

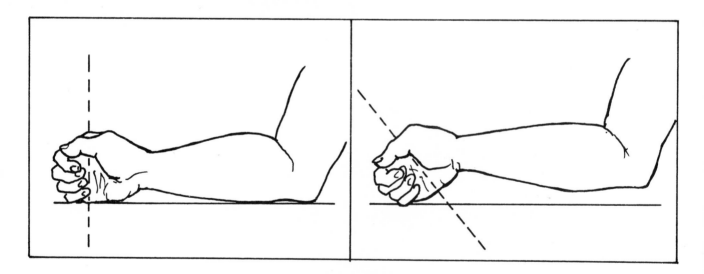

This exercise will incorporate another type of wrist action, a rocking motion of the cone. The bit will remain at the axis as the rest of the cone arcs forward or backward. To get the idea of this wrist action, place the right forearm on a table and make a fist with the thumb on top. Raise the elbow about an inch from the table and rock the fist forward on the little finger, not to the left or right, until the knuckles nearly touch the table top. This rocking motion with a decorating cone will allow the bit to follow the top contours of a bubble foundation. In forming sharp points at the tops of leaves and certain petals, the toe of the bit must contact the work surface, yet the heel must remain up on top of the foundation.

If the directions say, "rock the cone forward," this is the movement to be followed. Thus, when making the leaf (or a pointed petal), form the foundation of the leaf and keep the cone upright until it is midway up the forward stroke. At this position, as the tip begins its arc back to the "12 o'clock" position, start rocking the cone forward. At the tip of the leaf, the toe will be at "12 o'clock" and touching the work surface, but the heel will still be atop the bubble. Keep it rocked forward while beginning the "back up" stroke for the right side of the petal; gradually rock the cone back to perpendicular as the tip arcs to form the widest part of the petal. Let the bit rock back on its heel as it turns from "2 o'clock" back to "12 o'clock" on its downward path to complete the petal.

Situate the leaves around the ends of the stems in symmetrical clusters of threes, and fill in any remaining wide open spaces. Don't cover the area so completely that none of the background shows. These occasional open spaces also add to the depth to make the arrangement more free and natural.

170

ORCHID

It must be assumed at this point, that the student has given his fullest attention to the formation of each of the previously discussed flowers in this chapter. This is an absolute must before the reader attempts to make the orchid, as this one flower incorporates some of each of the interactions in the aforementioned exercises. Its long, slender petals described in "Part One" are longer and narrower than the dogwood leaf, but the pressure control and wrist action that this petal requires are much the same.

This exotic blossom is more complex than the other flowers, having three distinct parts. The first part consists of three petals that are structurally the same as the dogwood leaves, except that they are longer and more slender. The second part requires the placement of two shorter and very ruffled petals. The third part, the throat of the orchid, is a fluted bell at the end of a tube which extends from the center of the blossom.

172

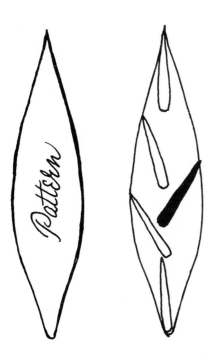

PART ONE OF ORCHID

Draw the outlined shape of this petal on tracing paper and observe the positions of the bit. The bubble for the foundation of this petal is long and rather narrow. It should begin less than three-fourths of an inch from the top point of the petal. Rock the cone backward as the bubble begins to build up, keeping the heel close to the surface, then straighten it to "perpendicular" to start the petal.

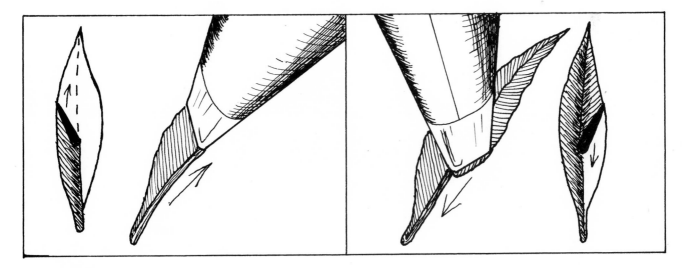

Shift the heel of the bit slightly to the right of the center line of the foundation and, with very little pressure, start the upward stroke that begins the petal. Make the ribbon of icing stretch as the cone arcs at the widest place, to a position between "10 and 11 o'clock." The pressure can be slightly increased while the tip is in this position, just enough to form the width of the petal, not

173

enough to cause the edge of the ribbon to droop. By this time the heel of the tip should have gradually moved left to the center line of the foundation, and from this moment should ride the center vein position. Continue the upward stroke, gradually arcing the bit back to the right while reducing the pressure and rocking the cone forward. At the top of the petal, the toe of the bit should be at "12 o'clock" and touching the work surface.

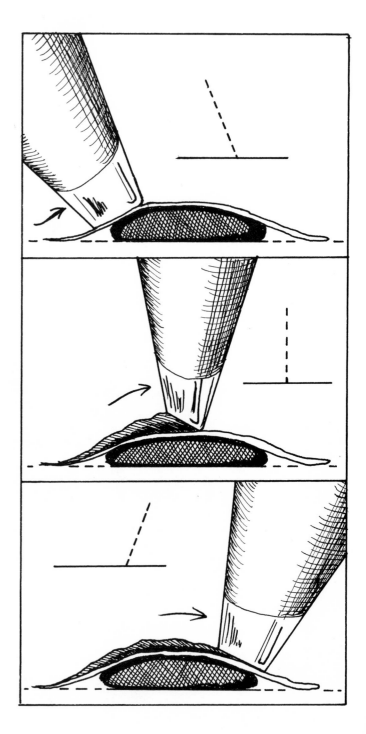

The heel should still be elevated and must remain in contact with the top of the foundation as the tip begins its downward stroke. Slowly rock the cone back to perpendicular, stretching the icing and arcing the tip to the right. From here, increase the pressure for a moment, then while relaxing it as the toe gently arcs back to narrow the petal, rock the cone back so that the toe is slightly raised. Rock the cone upright near the end of the downward stroke to sever the ribbon cleanly. The heel of the bit should ride straight down the center vein on the downward stroke, even overriding that part of the first petal which extends beyond the center.

Three of these petals will radiate symmetrically from a dot, like the spokes in a wheel; one of them pointed straight upward. They must not touch the center dot, but should gap enough to allow room to insert the throat section.

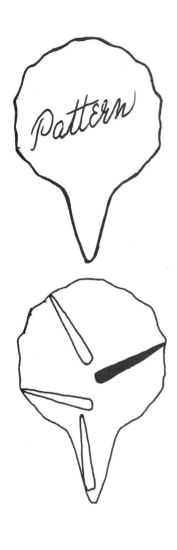

PART TWO OF ORCHID

This petal is narrow at the base, widening rather abruptly to a plume. The wide part is made with medium pressure and a jiggling motion, like the carnation petal.

Make an extra-full foundation for this petal. Begin the petal with the heel shifted to the right of the center line and with the bit barely arced so that its toe is just to the left of "12 o'clock." Hold this angle, stretching the ribbon for the first half-inch before arcing to almost "9 o'clock." Commence the jiggling motion as the tip pivots, and sustain this action to the top of the petal and down the other side until the petal narrows again. About a third of the way from the top, on the downward stroke, the cone should rock back on the heel to keep the petal from drooping because of the additional pressure and bulk. Allow it to straighten as the bit arcs back near the petal's base.

The two petals made in this manner will jut out from near the center dot at either side of, and adjacent to, the top petal described in "Part One." The margin between the two bottom petals will be occupied by the throat piece.

PART THREE OF ORCHID

This third and final section of the orchid is made on a specially shaped cardboard support which is inserted into a straw. The pattern for the cardboard support should be traced, folded on the dotted line, and cut to shape. Select a piece of cardboard about the thickness of the material from an ordinary cake box. Fold a piece that is large enough to fit within the folded paper pattern, and cut around the outline.

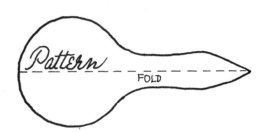

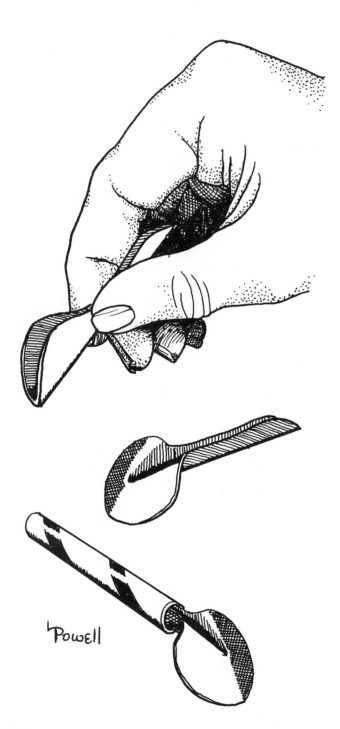

Hold the narrow shank of the *folded* support between the thumb and forefinger of the right hand, so that the folded edge is on the bottom and the pointed end is aimed at the palm. Allow the folded support to partially open, permitting the left thumb and forefinger to grip the round end, thumb on top and inside the fold. Ease the grip of the right hand to allow the front half of the circle to be bent downward.

Squeeze the narrow shank together and insert it, point down, into a piece of plastic straw (a large milkshake type, cut into thirds), so that the combined straw and cardboard form a rigid support for the orchid throat.

178

With the left thumb and forefinger, grasp the straw just below the position where it meets the cardboard. The open flap of cardboard should be aimed toward the decorator. Position the decorating tip with its heel at the center of the circular cardboard flap and with the toe aimed just to the right of the fold.

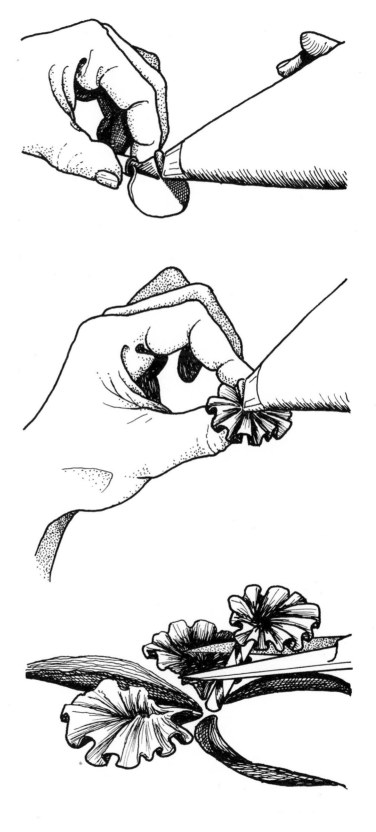

Fan a ruffled ribbon so that it completely encircles the cardboard flap. This ribbon should end at the left edge of the fold and must be completed with a firm burst of pressure as the tip is rocked back on its heel. Add a similar shape over the original starting position so that these two ends of the fan form a "V."

Position this throat section into the center of the blossom, allowing about an inch of the straw to penetrate the cake for support.

Hollow out the bell of the throat by slipping the point of a wet skewer down through the "V" where it meets the end of the straw. Turn the cake so that the throat section of the flower is aimed away and pipe a bead of icing down the exposed part of the straw. This bead of icing will resemble the foundation for one of the long petals. Finish the orchid by stippling the surface of the ruffled petals and throat with a small brush dipped into food color. Choose a dark color for these spots that will be in tasteful contrast to the hues of the flower. Deep purple on a lavender orchid, brown or golden yellow on a yellow or white blossom, and so on.

ORCHID BUD

The bud of the orchid is unfamiliar to the layman, because the orchid is primarily used as a full blossom in corsage form. Situate the orchid in a bed of rose buds, or add sprigs of lily of the valley or other tiny blossoms.

ORCHID FOLIAGE

If the orchid is in a corsage type arrangement with rose buds, use rose leaves for the background. In this case, lay out the stem design, arrange the leaves, then pipe on the orchid and cluster the rose buds around the perimeter.

Otherwise, the decorator can try creating a fern-like background, or experiment with other foliage varieties to find one that suits his or her own taste.

180

POINSETTIA

For most of the history of decorating, poinsettia petals have been formed mostly with leaf tips or star tips. When this flower is made with a rose tip, it takes on a really life-like appearance. The individual petals are formed much like the pointed ones in "Part One" of the orchid but they narrow more abruptly at their tips. The poinsettia has two layers of petals; the first is as simple to form with a Number 125 rose tip as are the leaves and petals for other flowers. The second layer is more difficult and its smaller petals may require extra practice. These secondary petals can also be made with the Number 125 rose tip; however, more satisfactory results may be achieved if one uses a Number 104 rose tip. This tip will allow greater control and will produce a lighter weight petal that is less likely to crush the lower ones.

ARRANGE THE FIRST LAYER OF PETALS

Arrange the six long petals about a center dot, making certain to leave a margin between them and the dot. This blossom will have even greater realism and interest if it is piped within an imaginary oval. This oval shape helps to make the poinsettia appear to be at an angle to the observer, much as he would view it in a natural arrangement. When the flower is created perfectly round, it presents the impression that the observer is standing directly over it, and this position would seem awkward.

ARRANGE THE SECOND LAYER OF PETALS

Examine the illustration carefully before attempting to add the second layer of smaller petals. The petals in this layer are staggered in length, and each starts with the marginal distance from the dot, but not necessarily between two petals of the first row. Begin a secondary petal directly over a primary petal then angle it slightly to one side so that it does not completely fill the open space between the first petals. This is to achieve the openness discussed in earlier compositions. Also, each secondary petal will be formed over a foundation which is thinner than, but similar to, the one for the larger petal.

This time, however, it will not always be possible to rock the cone until the toe touches the cake or work surface, so the upward stroke will stop with the toe in mid-air and with the heel still in contact with the top of the foundation. To start the downward stroke, it will be necessary to use pressure, rather than to stretch the ribbon. If the petal doesn't maintain a sharp point after it has been completed, gently touch it with a glancing, upward stroke with the side of the decorating tip.

The center of the poinsettia is like a cluster of tiny berries or seeds. Stripe a plain cone like the one for dogwood, only with stripes of red and green, then fill it with light yellow. Pipe a large bubble in the center of the flower about a quarter-inch in diameter, then cover it with the tiny beads of icing.

POINSETTIA FOLIAGE

The leaves of the poinsettia are just like the petals. Pipe them on in much the same manner as the dogwood leaves, but use three to five leaves in each cluster. For interesting variations, arrange the blossoms with other seasonal foliage like holly with its rich red berries, or over clusters of pine boughs with or without pine cones.

182

PART ONE OF DAFFODIL

An arrangement of these natural looking daffodils will bring a touch of springtime to any cake they adorn. Each blossom is made in two parts. The first part is formed on the cake over the foliage arrangement and is composed of six yellow petals in a design like the spokes of a wheel. The second part is an inverted bell formed over a segment of plastic drinking straw that will be inserted into the cake at the center of the "wheel." This bell may be formed from the same color as the petals or may be piped in yellow-orange tones.

PART ONE

These petals are similar to the petals of the poinsettia. They should be as small as can possibly be made with a Number 125 rose tip. It is not necessary that the ends of these petals should come to a sharp point; therefore, avoid touching the toe of the decorating tip to the work surface at the end of the upward stroke. Instead, use a little extra pressure to start the downward motion on the second half of the petal. The six petals should be assembled so that they do not touch at the center of the wheel to allow sufficient space to insert the bell.

PART TWO OF DAFFODIL

The inverted bell in the center of the flower is formed with a Number 125 rose tip over a quarter-length of plastic milk-shake straw. Its outermost rim is ruffled much like the carnation petal.

Hold a quarter-length of straw in the left hand as for making the pine cone. Encircle the top of the straw with a band of icing. To do this, position the tip so that the top of the ribbon will be a little above the end of the straw, and allow the ribbon to wrap around about one and a half turns.

Start the top ruffled portion of the bell by fastening the ribbon below the foundation and by moving the tip straight upward until its heel is above the center of the previously formed band. Now, turn the straw while jiggling the cone until the ruffled bell overlaps at its starting place. End with a downward stroke, twisting the wrist slightly clockwise so that the toe of the bit touches into the icing for a cut-off finish.

Add a third band of icing, with the toe touching into the base of the ruffled band, so that the foundation has at least a double thickness of ribbon. Make the top of the last band blend as smoothly as possible with the bottom of the second, so that the sides of the bell will not appear to be ragged.

Use scissors for support at the base of the bell to help to position the flower into the cake. Insert the straw stem so that the bell angles slightly away from the center of interest.

DAFFODIL BUD

Buds for the daffodil are long and slender, just like the petals. Use a narrow version of one of these petals for a new bud, or cluster several petals for a more open bud.

DAFFODIL FOLIAGE

The leaves for the daffodil are narrow and long, similar to the carnation leaves, but straighter. Make them with a cone cut to a leaf tip, of a size smaller than that for a rose leaf. Angle the leaves away from the point of interest so that their formation suggests the shape of the complete arrangement. Since the daffodil is rather large compared to a rose, use only three blossoms for a smaller cake.

CHAPTER V
Anatomy: Drawing and Figure Piping

Anatomy: Drawing and Figure Piping

LEARN TO DRAW THE HUMAN FIGURE

This study will include basic lessons in drawing the human body and many animals. The primary concern will be the human figure, its proportions, balance, and action. Particular emphasis will be placed on facial details.

The best way to learn is to practice drawing each of the figures. Decorating students who swear they've never been able to draw will soon discover they can make unusually realistic, well-proportioned faces and figures with just a little practice. Faithful practice of this exercise is extremely important for those who are sincerely interested in becoming adept at figure piping. Like those for composition, there are generally accepted formulas for proportioning the human figure.

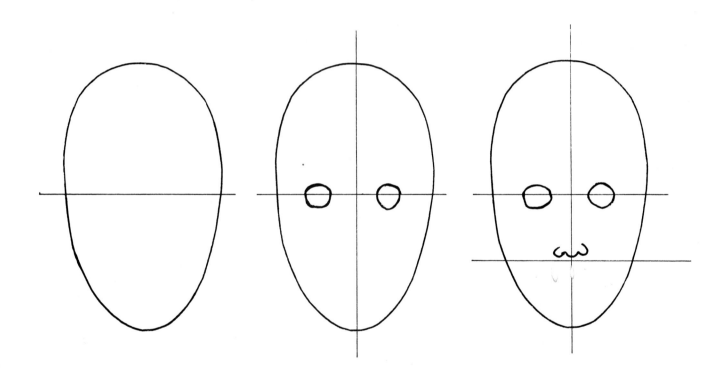

THE HEAD

Draw the outline of an egg on a piece of paper. Position it so that the small part of the oval is at the bottom. Pencil in light lines to divide the egg, horizontally and vertically, into halves. The horizontal line will mark the position on the face for the eyes. Divide the lower half of the face with another light horizontal line, halfway between the center line and the bottom of the egg. The tip of the nose will extend down nearly to this line.

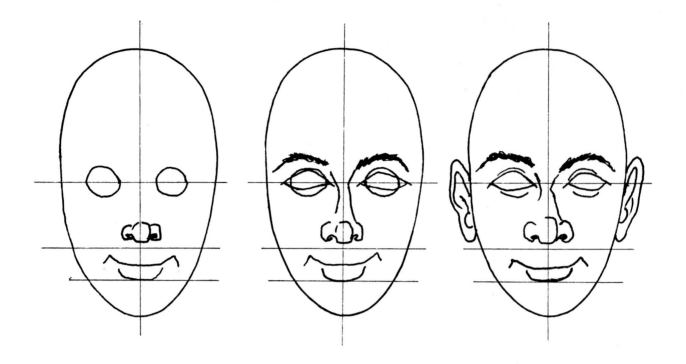

Draw the lower lip at a line about midway between the tip of the nose and the bottom of the egg, or the chin line. Position eyebrows just over the eyes and indicate the shapes of the nose and lips.

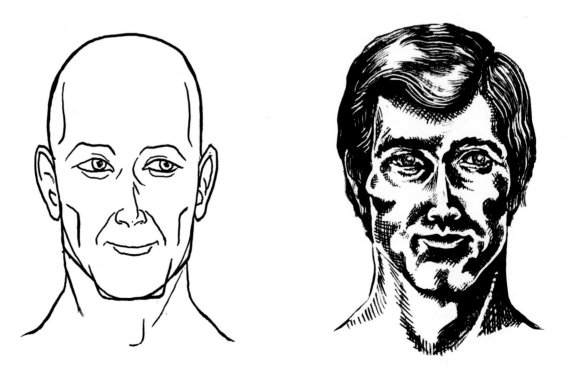

To draw the head in more detail, it will be necessary to look at the human skull and to learn its shape and its features. Study the domed shape that houses the brain, and note its general position and its contours. At its widest part, on the sides, the back of the skull is slightly wider than the forehead. The temple area between the eyes and the ears, just above the cheek bone, is slightly concave.

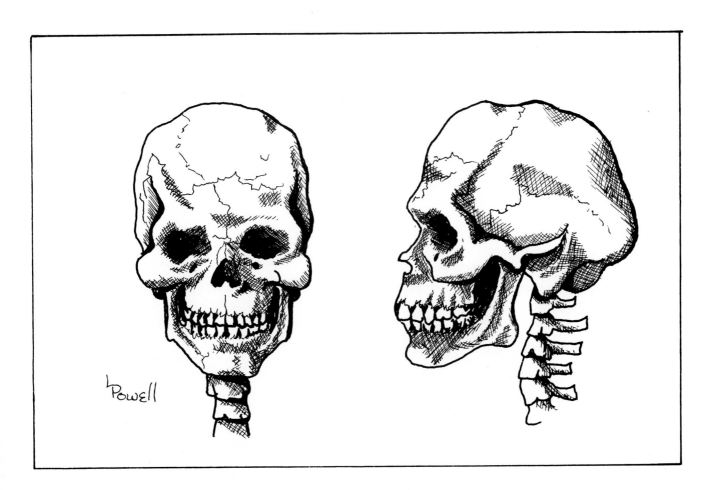

The profile shows the angles of the front teeth, and one can see how they affect the shape of the mouth. The sockets that house the eyes are set deeply into the skull, and the eyes are protected by the brow line and the cheek bones. The spine connects at a central position below the skull to balance the structure.

The additional contours of the face are supplied by formations of cartilage and muscles. Generally though, the main shape of the head is dependent on the actual structure of the skull. The nose is mostly cartilage, and its size and shape have probably more influence on a person's appearance than does any other feature.

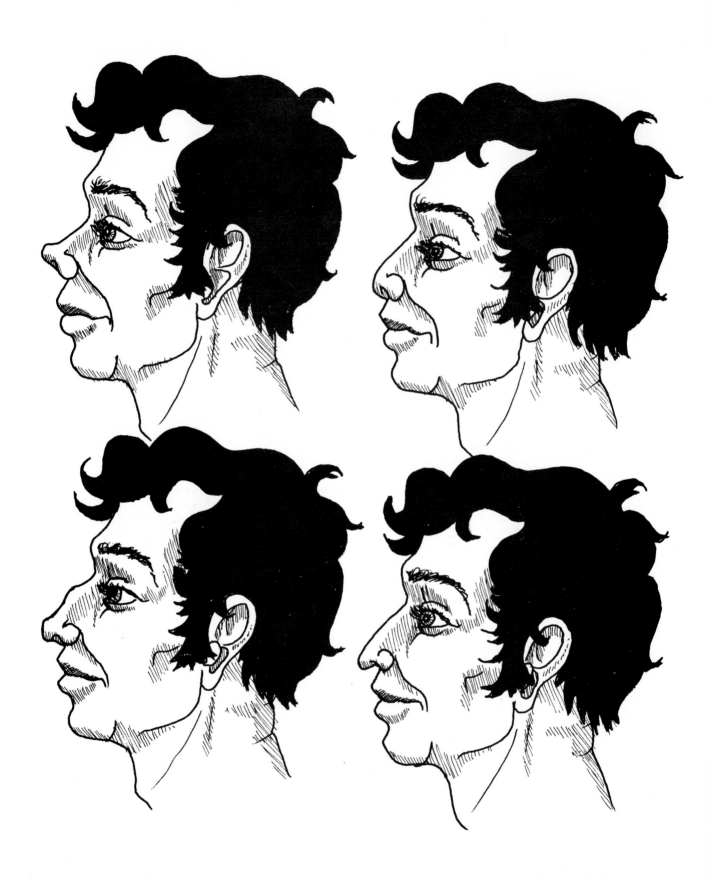

To point out how one feature can affect the individuality of a face, the illustration shows a series of profiles; each one exactly the same, except for the nose.

192

Another distinguishing characteristic is the shape of the hair style, the hair line, or the absence of hair. Make sure that the hair style complements and even emphasizes the age and the personality of the figure.

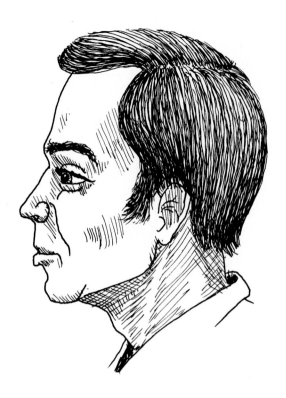

The egg shape is nearly accurate for the proportions of the head of a mature adult, but the skull takes on different shapes and contours in direct relation to age. By comparative proportions, the size of the skull increases least of almost any other bone in the body. Therefore, from infancy to adulthood, the rest of the body usually more than triples its size, while the head grows a relatively small amount.

The child's head is not such a tall oval as is the adult's, but it is deeper from front to back, and the protecting surfaces around the eye sockets are not so well developed. The lower front of the skull protrudes in the region of the mouth and teeth. The chin, nose and ears are not fully formed.

The skull of a more elderly man or woman again decreases in height, and the domed portion shifts slightly back and downward. As the chin is more dominant, the mouth takes on a slight concave turn. The eyes are set deeper into the head, and often the nose angles downward, bulging slightly at the bridge where the cartilage meets the bone.

194

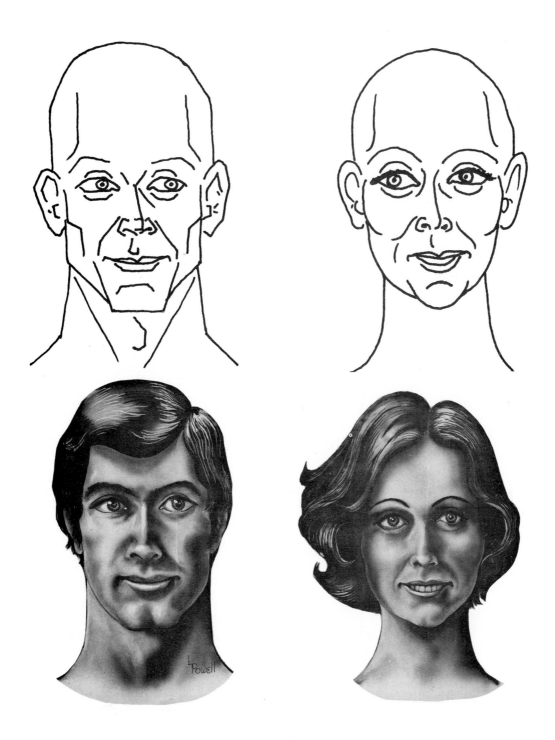

The lines in a man's face are bold and the features are more square. The typical woman's face is composed of softer lines. For instance, the chin is smaller and more nearly round, and the smile lines from the sides of the nose to the corners of the mouth are not so deep and obvious.

Although there are structural guide rules for the average placement of features on a face, individuality prevails. When one considers all the faces in the world, he is aware that there are few look-alikes. Each face is distinctly different from the next. In a portrait, an artist carefully makes use of these distinctions. He must be aware of the shape and size of each feature and of its relationship to another, as well as of its approximation to the average position on a face.

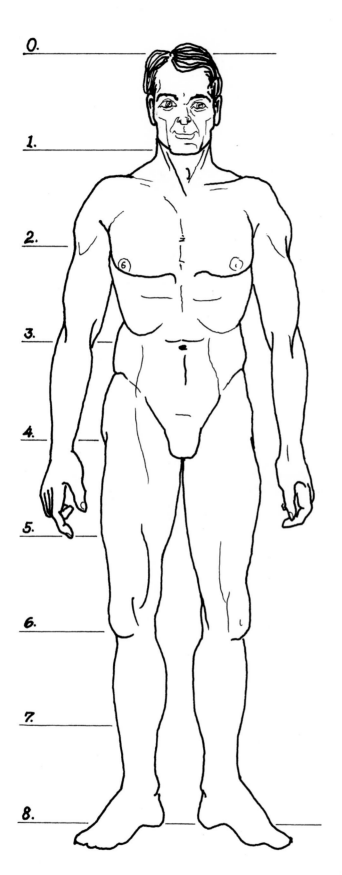

0.

1.

2.

3.

4.

5.

6.

7.

8.

PROPORTIONS OF THE HUMAN FIGURE

The figure is comprised of certain primary forms: the head, spine (neck and backbone), trunk (rib cage or chest and pelvis), arms (upper and lower), hands, legs (upper and lower), and feet.

The ideal proportions for an adult male are more easily understood when the figure is marked off into eight equal segments from top to bottom. The head extends from the top down to Line One. The shoulders, at the top of the trunk, are just above midway between Line One and Line Two. The measurement across the chest is approximately equal to two head widths and the bottom of the rib cage extends to just above Line Three. The pelvis extends from below Line Three down to Line Four. Take special note that the position where the legs meet at the base of the trunk (the crotch) is at the exact center of the figure. The legs actually fasten at the hip joints on each side of the pelvis at about a quarter segment above the center line. The base of each knee rests on Line Six, halfway between the crotch and heels. The ankles are at a position not quite half a segment up from the bottom line. The elbows are nearly in line with the top of the pelvis. The tips of the fingers, when the arms are relaxed at the sides of the body, should extend nearly to Line Five.

The best method for learning to draw a well-proportioned human figure is for the student first to practice sketching the block form with a pencil and paper. Draw two lines across the paper to determine the height of the figure: one line near the upper edge to indicate the top of the head; the other near the bottom of the paper to mark the position for the bottom of the heels. Divide the space between these two lines into eight equal segments.

Try to keep the width of the body in proportion to its height, as nearly like the illustration as possible. Beginners sometimes find it difficult, in their first attempts, to keep the figure perfectly vertical. If this is a problem, draw a light vertical line to indicate the center of the body before drawing the figure.

After repeated practice the student should become sufficiently familiar with the proper shapes and proportions so that he can consistently draw the block figure without using guide lines. Carefully scrutinize each completed figure. If it is not just right, compare it with this illustration and circle portions of the sketch that need correction. Concentrate on the circled areas to improve succeeding sketches.

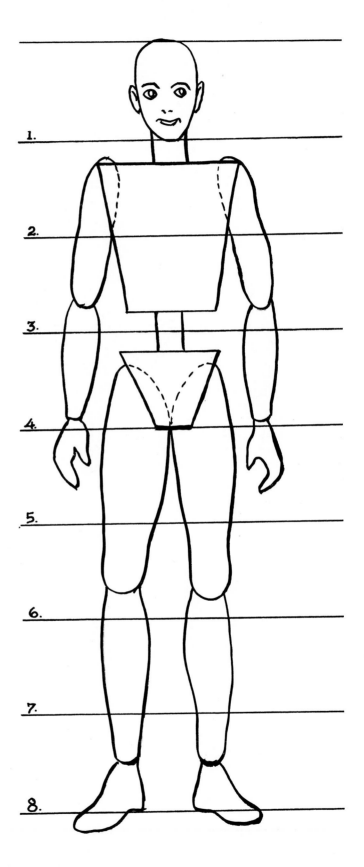

197

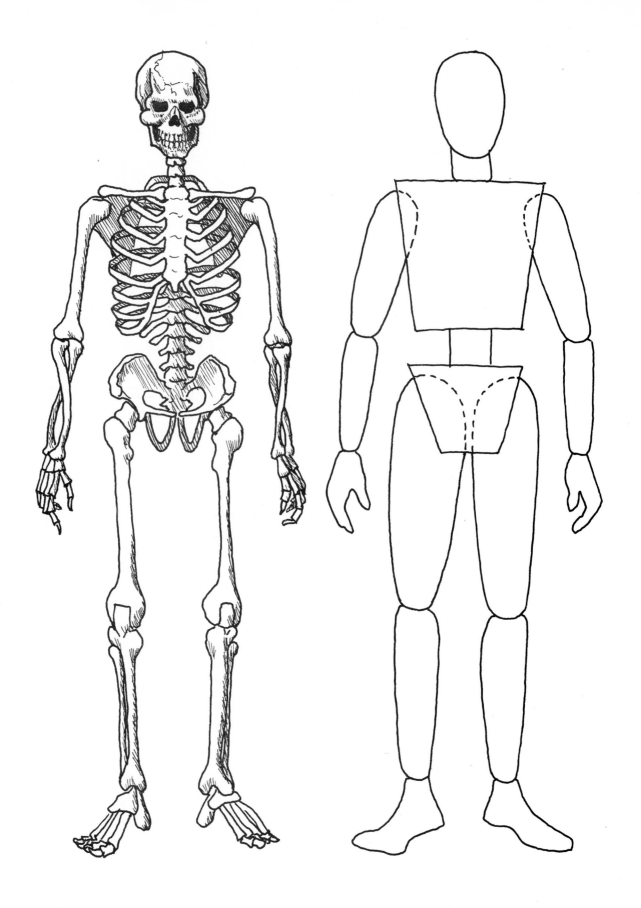

Compare the block figure with the shapes and positions of the bones of the skeleton. Learn the position of the bones to draw more accurately shaped figures.

198

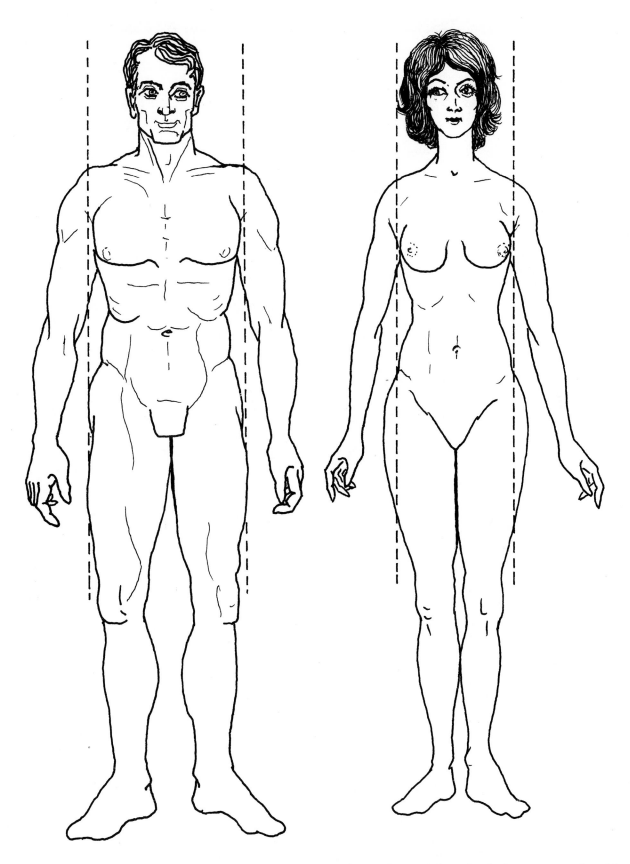

The most important structural differences between the male and female skeletons are shoulder and pelvic widths. The man's hips are only slightly wider than the bottom of his rib cage; where-as, the woman's hips are wide in comparison to her petite chest and narrow shoulders.

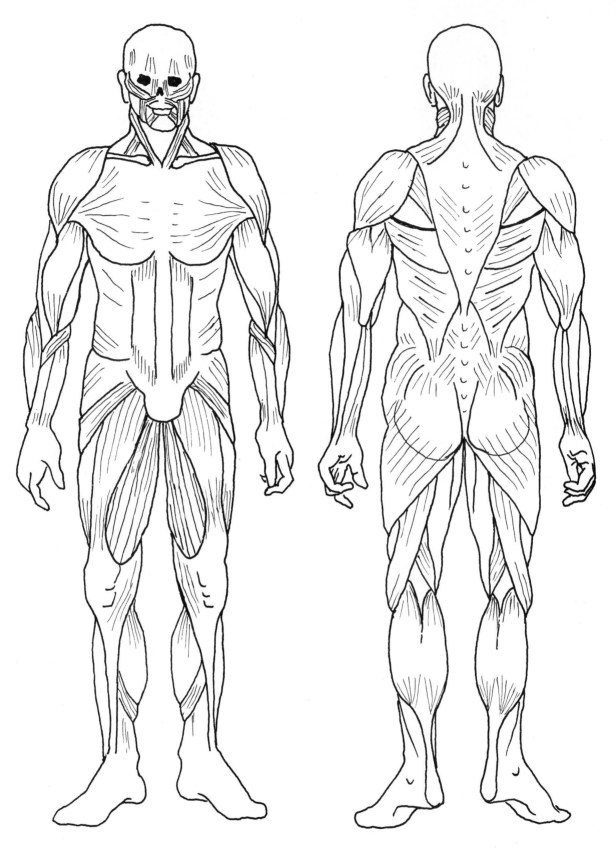

Become familiar with the shapes of the major muscle formations and with their positions on the skeletal framework. A man's muscles, compared to those of most women, are heavier and more developed in the legs and arms. The abdominal region between his chest and pelvis is also more padded.

200

The neck of a male figure is large, nearly as wide as his jaws, and it reveals the mastoid muscle that connects behind the ears and runs down to the collar bone. These muscles will be less prominent in the neck of the female. The collar bone will appear as a definite ridge on both the man and the woman.

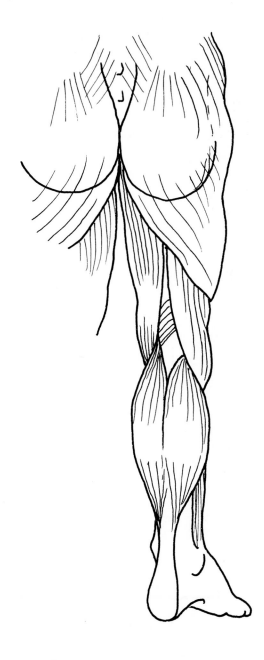

The calf muscle at the back of the lower leg is bulky, and it pads the back side of the bones. The main bone (tibia) is very near the front surface of the leg. This bone, and the muscle tissues that cover it, form a ridge extending from the knee to the inner side of the ankle. The bone in the upper leg is well padded on the front and back. A large muscle pads the upper back side of the leg, near the hip, and forms the cheek of the buttock and provides protection for the base of the spine.

201

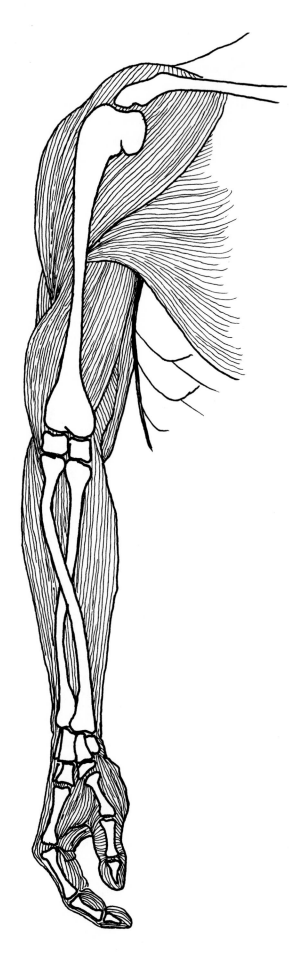
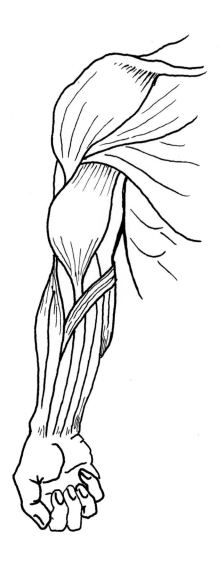

The bone in the upper arm is padded on the top and bottom, but the bicep muscle on the top is larger. The padding on the lower arm is fastened on the outer and the inner sides of the bones, instead of above and below.

The hand and fingers are formed from a very flexible network of bones. The hand is well padded on the palm side with muscles that provides its general formation. The undersides of the fingers are padded too, but the bones are primarily responsible for their shape.

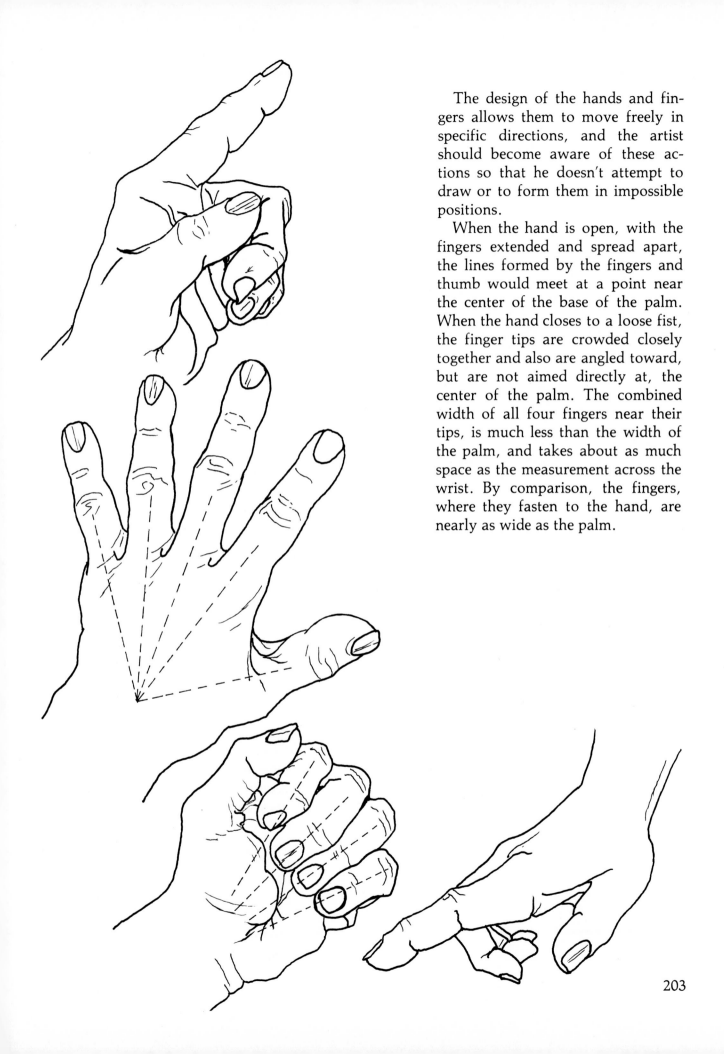

The design of the hands and fingers allows them to move freely in specific directions, and the artist should become aware of these actions so that he doesn't attempt to draw or to form them in impossible positions.

When the hand is open, with the fingers extended and spread apart, the lines formed by the fingers and thumb would meet at a point near the center of the base of the palm. When the hand closes to a loose fist, the finger tips are crowded closely together and also are angled toward, but are not aimed directly at, the center of the palm. The combined width of all four fingers near their tips, is much less than the width of the palm, and takes about as much space as the measurement across the wrist. By comparison, the fingers, where they fasten to the hand, are nearly as wide as the palm.

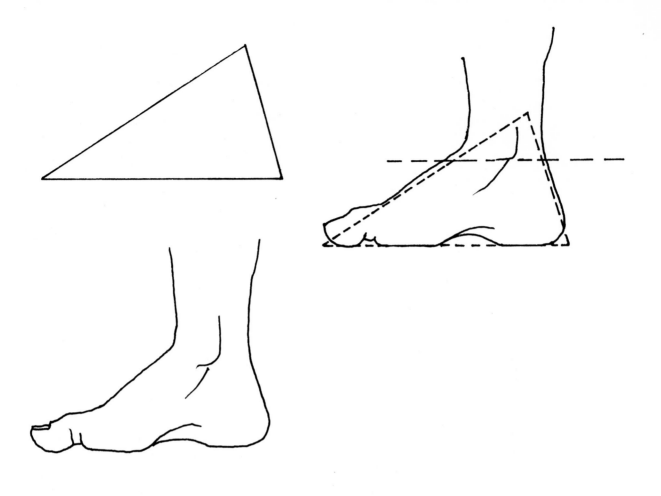

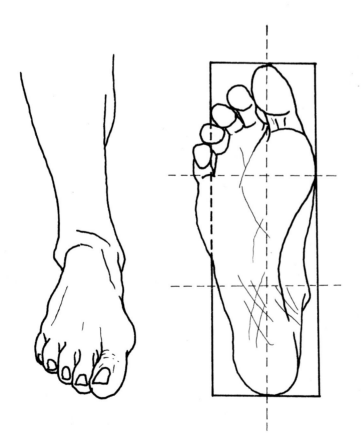

Basically, the foot is a wedge that fastens to the tubular formation for the leg. This tube and wedge overlap, so that the base of the leg fastens to the foot at a position about one-third of the way down from the highest point of the wedge, to form the ankle joint. Therefore, when drawing or piping the foot in different positions, one must always take into consideration that the foot is allowed to pivot forward or backward at this joint. Figure piping does not generally require the decorator to employ a great amount of detail in the formation of the foot. However, it is important that one must be aware of the basic shape and mobility of the foot so that its proportions and its positions are relative to the figure.

BALANCE

Balance is a key factor when one is drawing or piping a figure. If the form is not properly balanced, even a person with an untrained eye will realize that something is wrong. The observer may not be able to put his finger on the problem but he will definitely feel uncomfortable about the position into which the artist has forced the figure. In cake decorating or in drawing, the artist must deal with two basic types of figures: one kind is supported on two legs, the other stands with its weight distributed on four. This study will mostly be concerned with the first type, and will include humans as well as cartoon style animals.

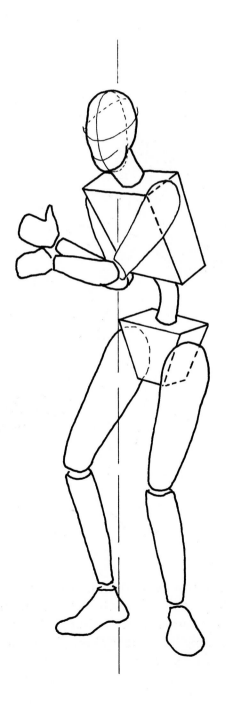

When a figure is relatively still and standing erectly, the head and chest should either be balanced directly over one foot or over a point midway between the positions of the two feet. If the figure bends at the waist, the buttocks must lean backward to counterbalance the weight of the head.

MOTION

When the figure is on the move, but drawn as though the artist had captured the motion for a moment, the HEAD AND CHEST should be leading in that direction which the body is traveling. Even in this position, some of the weight will be balanced by an arm or a leg, or by both, extended in the opposite direction.

The actions for running and walking are initiated by the movement of the feet and legs. The arms provide balance and, where speed is concerned, thrust. When the left leg moves forward, the left arm swings backward; at the same time, the right arm is reaching ahead to maintain proper balance. The arms move freely like the swinging of a pendulum. Most of this action results from the twisting motion and the shifting angle of the shoulders.

206

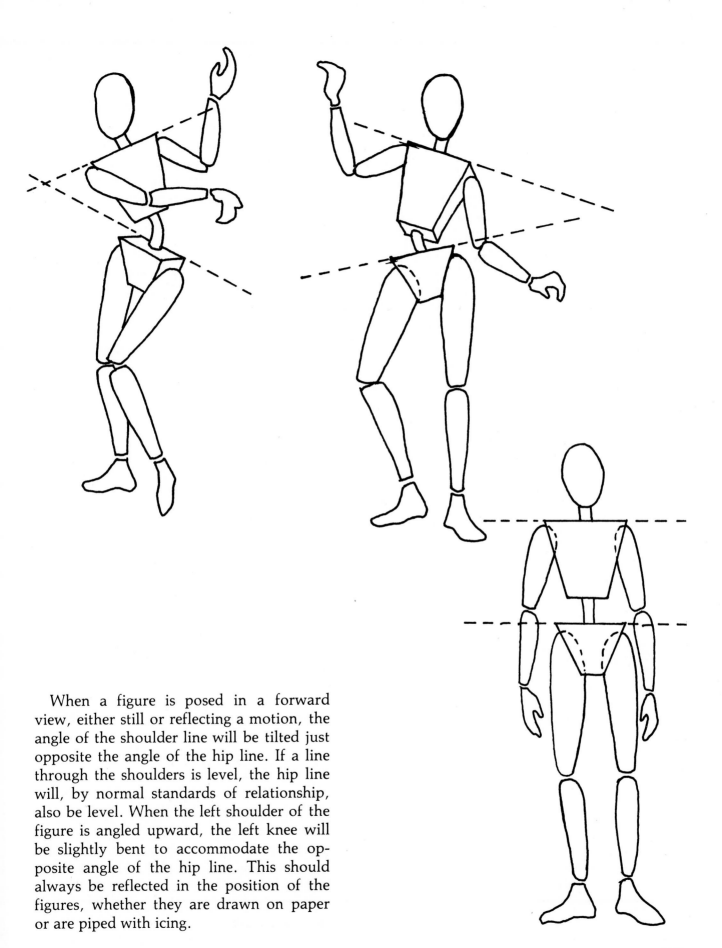

When a figure is posed in a forward view, either still or reflecting a motion, the angle of the shoulder line will be tilted just opposite the angle of the hip line. If a line through the shoulders is level, the hip line will, by normal standards of relationship, also be level. When the left shoulder of the figure is angled upward, the left knee will be slightly bent to accommodate the opposite angle of the hip line. This should always be reflected in the position of the figures, whether they are drawn on paper or are piped with icing.

LEARN TO DRAW ANIMALS

With nature's endless variety, it is difficult for any artist to remember the shapes and the proportions of more than a few animals. Where the human anatomy dealt primarily with a single set of proportions, each specie in the family of animals has its own set of blueprints. Consider just the "cat" family: there must be dozens of domestic breeds, not to mention lions, tigers, cougars, bobcats, chetahs, leopards, and the list goes on and on. Most artists depend on live models and photos for sketching specific animals. Each decorating student should include a good selection of animal pictures in his files for ready reference. The very best sources are the many drawing books which are available at art supply stores. Anyone who hopes to specialize in figure piping must be familiar with the generally most popular animals. Those which are requested most frequently for cakes include: horses, dogs, cats, and various circus animals. The only way for any student to increase his familiarity with these general categories is to sketch them as often as is possible. This will require careful study of pictures and of live animals (whenever possible), and careful analysis of the details of each body. This text will attempt to provide only a generalized introduction to a few animals with the hope that this sample will pique the curiosity of the reader, inspire his interest, and will make him more aware of the important details that one must absorb in order to become a better decorator.

Animal bodies are composed of formations similar to those that make up the human anatomy. Their skeletons include the skull, rib cage, pelvis, spinal column, and legs (the forelegs are comparable to man's arms). When drawing an animal, an artist must examine and analyze the shapes and positions of the bones in the skeleton and then should translate them into block formations. Each student can utilize the experience gained from drawing the human figure to help him to make an accurate analysis.

Study the drawings on the opposite page and compare the block formations of the man and dog. When man is positioned as though he were walking on all fours, he is more aware of the structural similarities that he shares with the animal world. Although there is a basic likeness, their proportions and features give each form its own peculiar identity. An artist's ability is determined by how successfully he is able to interpret these proportions and the details of individual features.

BALANCE AND MOTION

An earlier discussion in this chapter was devoted to balance and motion as they applied either to man or to cartoon figures. Animals that stand on four legs have greater stability and this changes the balance factor—the body weight, in this case, is distributed evenly over all four limbs. Having recognized the comparisons of man's arms to forelegs and of his legs to the hind legs of other creatures, one can more easily understand motion as it applies to animals. For most sketching and cake decorating purposes, the artist will be concerned with two characteristic actions: a normal walking pace and a high speed run.

In the normal walking pace, the animal's forelegs and hind legs assume the same pattern of motion as those demonstrated by the arms and legs of man. Thus, the hind legs of the animal provide the impetus for all of its motions. When the left hind leg moves forward, the right foreleg swings ahead to support and to balance the weight of the body.

High speed running motion is best expressed by long, leaping strides in which the animal's back arches to allow both hind legs to move forward simultaneously. When its hind feet reach ahead, the forelegs are thrust back beneath the animal's body. As soon as the hind feet make contact with the ground, they act as a catapult to push the body forward and the back straightens as the forelegs reach ahead to grasp for more footing. Not only the animal's legs, but its whole anatomy reflects the speed as he leaps ahead. The head and neck stretch forward and the ears lie back.

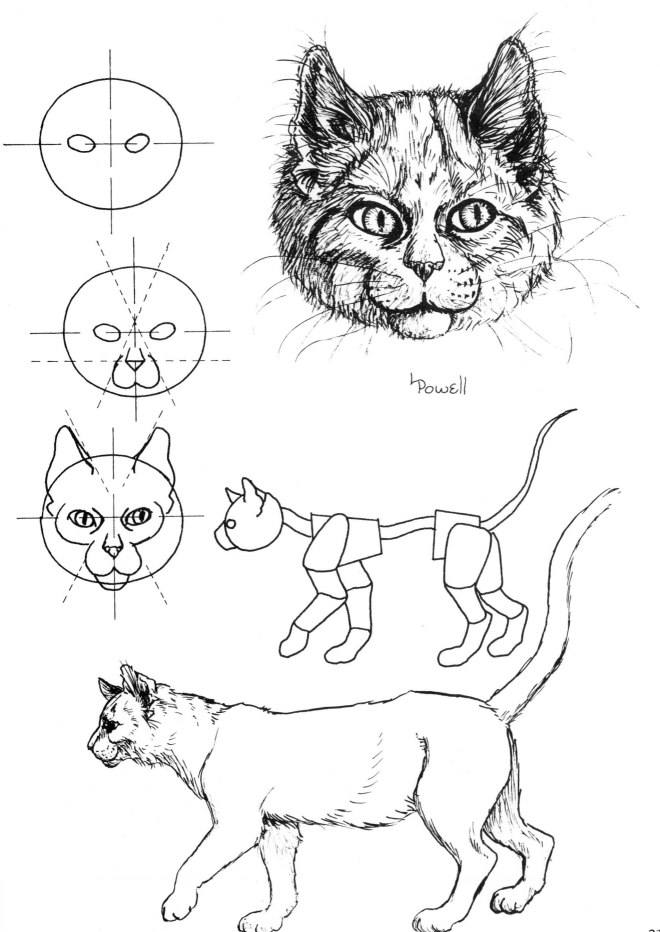

Powell

Powell

212

Powell

FIGURE PIPING

Throughout the first part of this chapter, the emphasis has been on learning to analyze proportions and shapes of human and animal body structures, and on how to translate them into block sketches. Through figure piping, a decorator retranslates those sketches into three dimensional icing forms. The degree of his success depends greatly on how skillfully he can control pressure and manipulate the decorating cone.

FORMATIONS MUST BE SMOOTH

Strive to make smooth formations. The first requirement is, of course, to begin with properly mixed buttercream. Fresh buttercream will at first be soft and creamy. It will perform more satisfactorily after it has aged for a day or more. Decorating buttercream should never be refrigerated! Refrigeration will break down the components of the icing to such an extent that its elastic properties will be destroyed. Once the icing is divided into smaller containers and is mixed to selected hues with paste food color, aeration is easily controlled. Eliminate excess air bubbles by stirring the buttercream with a bowl knife or wooden spoon. The icing should be stirred each time before it is used to fill a decorating cone, in order to insure the smoothest formations. A freshly filled cone for beginning each figure will give the most desirable results. If a decorating cone is allowed to remain unused for even a short period, its contents will start to become aerated.

Powell

Smoothness is a result of sustained pressure coupled with steady motion. The decorator must be able to coordinate the two. Before he attempts to pipe figures, he should become thoroughly familiar with the primary techniques. This can only be done with experience and, therefore, requires careful, concentrated practice by each student.

The final smoothing process is accomplished by brushing the figures with the soft bristles of an artist's paint brush that has been dampened with hot water. In order to reduce the brushing time, it is very important that the decorator make the buttercream figure as nearly smooth and as perfectly shaped as he possibly can. Otherwise crucial minutes will be squandered, and "figure piping" will become a nonproductive form of decorating because of the wasted motions. Indeed, one cannot hope to acquire adequate speed if he does not learn to pipe *smooth* figures.

LEARN FIRST THINGS, FIRST

Early in life, each student learned to read, write, add, and subtract. He also learned to recognize the shape and identity of each letter and numerical symbol. Granted, the process didn't follow that order, but that is the whole point—the reason for making a comparison of the elementary learning procedures of "grammar school" to the study of figure piping. The learning sequence must be logical and should follow orderly patterns with "first things, first." That process, as it applies to figure piping, has already begun. The progressive studies throughout this book from its earliest pages have been organized to prepare the reader with the necessary guide lines and, if he has applied them with experimentation and practice, the training that he needs in order to control and to manipulate a decorating cone skillfully.

The elementary formations that follow are as important to learning figure piping as are the A B C's to learning reading and writing. Why are they important? Because each formation is a separate component. Each depends on specific movements and on accurate control of the decorating cone for its proper shape. These basic icing formations include long cylindrical columns, round bubbles, teardrops, and a variety of other controlled shapes. All the components are simple, but they require concentration and practice before they can be combined to produce figures that can be piped on a cake with confidence and ease. To proceed with figure piping without preliminary practice of these formations would be a great waste of valuable time. Not only would it take extra time to learn the "art" but the student would likely become so discouraged with his efforts that he might give up in defeat. Don't try to do it the hard way!

The only way anyone can acquire and perfect the skills of figure piping is for him to learn exactly how to control the flow of buttercream. This control is affected by four things: (1) the size of the opening in the decorating cone, (2) the amount of pressure exerted to force the icing from the cone, (3) the speed at which the decorating cone is moved, and (4) the distance that the tip of the decorating cone is allowed to rise above the work surface.

The figures in this book will, for the most part, be piped with plain parchment decorating cones with their tips cut to different-sized openings. Some openings will be small enough to pipe string-sized lines and others will range to diameters comparable to the width of one's little finger; each size will have its own limitations. Each cone must be carefully cut with sharp scissors to provide the smoothest possible opening—any rough flaps or notches in the cone's tip will prevent a smooth flow of icing.

Following is a series of exercises, accompanied by photographs. Carefully read the directions, then practice each exercise with buttercream. Use a parchment cone with its tip cut to a quarter-inch opening. The student should repeatedly practice with this cone until he becomes totally aware of its limitations.

Since limitations do exist, one cannot depend on a single-sized decorating cone for all of his needs. It is important that the decorator broaden his awareness of how other decorating cones perform with openings of different sizes. The only way that this can be accomplished is by experimentation. Fill a new parchment cone, and cut a small tip. After practicing each exercise with this cone, fill another, cut a larger opening and repeat the same formations. All the while, the student should be making every effort to perfect his skills in shaping. These experiments should lead each decorator to explore the effects of a variety of opening sizes before he attempts to combine the buttercream forms to pipe either comic or realistic likenesses of people or animals.

Pressure and speed combine to affect the size and the shape of a formation. When the decorating cone is moved in a straight line across the work surface, the icing, under steady pressure, will form a cylindrical column.

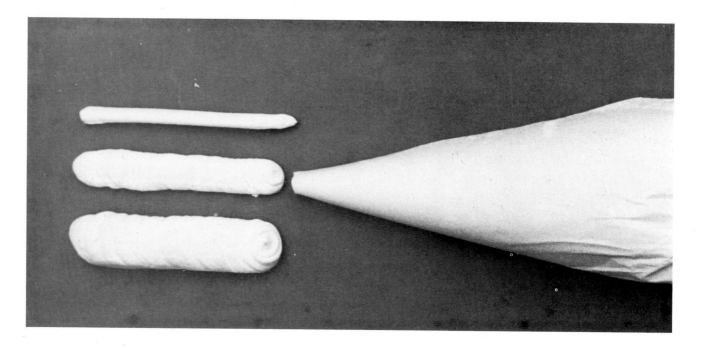

CYLINDRICAL COLUMN

Apply pressure and move the decorating cone in a straight line. Under gentle pressure, the size of this formation will be nearly the same as the opening in the decorating cone. With stronger pressure, the size of such a column can be increased. By increasing the pressure and moving the cone at a slower speed, one can easily double the diameter of a column without cutting a larger opening. For the larger columns, the tip of the cone must be allowed to rise higher above the work surface to accommodate the greater volume of icing.

BUBBLE

To form a bubble, start the flow of icing and allow the tip of the decorating cone to rise atop the form. As the form deepens, apply more pressure and slow the rising action of the cone until the desired diameter for the bubble is achieved. Gradually relax the pressure as the cone is lifted to complete a nearly round ball.

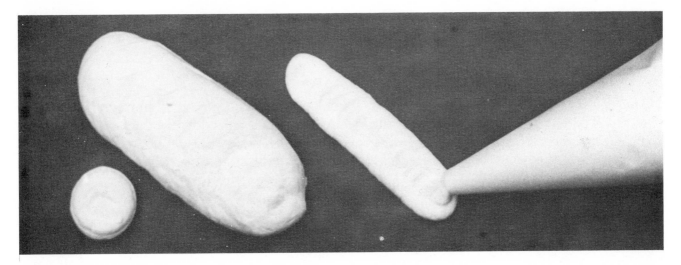

FLAT COLUMN

The flat column is similar to the cylindrical column but, as its name implies, it is wider and flatter. Begin with the same procedure as for piping a bubble, only control the rise of the cone so that its tip is lifted just enough to gain a desirable depth. The depth of this form is left entirely to the judgment of the decorator, and can obviously be controlled by either lifting or lowering the tip of the decorating cone. Start the bubble, then raise the tip slowly while exerting enough pressure to force the icing formation to a diameter that seems appropriate for the intended width of the column. Begin moving the decorating cone, maintaining whatever speed and pressure are necessary to sustain that width until the flat column is completed. This exercise will help the student to understand the results that one can obtain by changing the height of the decorating cone's tip in relation to the work surface.

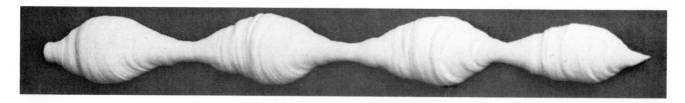

THICK AND THIN COLUMN

The thick and thin column is a study in pressure control. The decorating cone is moved in a straight line while the decorator alternately increases and decreases the pressure. It may be necessary to slow the speed of movement where the column widens to allow the icing's volume to build sufficiently. This important exercise will probably be the most beneficial of all, as some form of its application is used in nearly every piped figure.

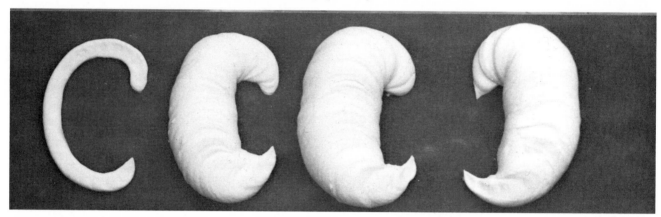

"C" FORMATION

The "C" formation is like a section of the "thick and thin" column. It is simply a forward or reversed "C" that begins with slight pressure and builds to a considerable thickness at its mid-section, then narrows as it starts its upward curl to complete the stroke.

TEARDROP

Teardrop shapes are like the individual segments of a shell border. Each begins with a bubble, but the decorating cone is moved away from its starting position as the pressure is simultaneously relaxed to taper the form to a point.

A similar shape may be piped in reverse, however it requires great concentration and practice in order to master a controlled, smooth form that graduates from a thin point and expands to full size. It must originate with very light pressure and as the decorating cone is moved, the pressure must be carefully increased so that the formation expands with the fewest possible ripples.

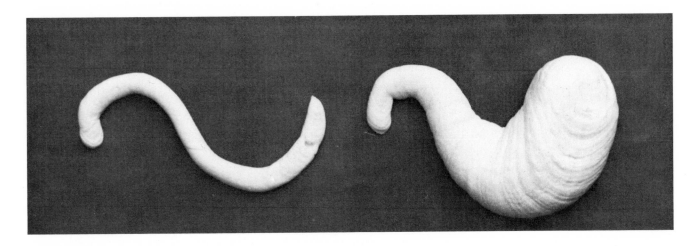

TAPERED "S"

The tapered "S" formation is an adaptation of the reversed teardrop. This is a backward "S" piped in a horizontal position. This exercise can be more easily learned if, at first, the student practices the curved lines without concentrating on pressure control. After he becomes accustomed to the necessary movements, the decorator can then give proper attention to applying the gradually increasing pressure as he did to form the reversed teardrop.

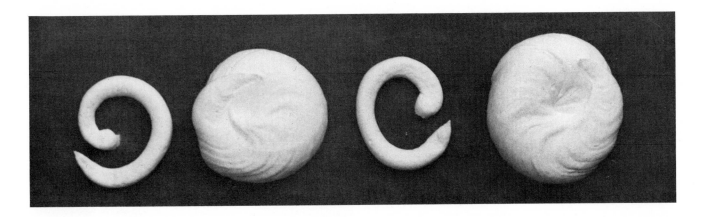

SWIRL BUBBLE

The "swirl bubble" is employed whenever it is more desirable to make a larger formation than the ordinary bubble that one can achieve without changing to a decorating cone with a larger opening. It is a swirl of icing, piped with heavy pressure, and may be formed either clockwise or counterclockwise. Once the decorator has determined the size of the bubble that he desires, he must pipe a circle of icing comparable to that size, using as much pressure as the tip's opening will allow. Without relaxing the pressure, as the circle's full circumference has been reached, the swirling motion should be continued so that the icing is spiraled inward to completely fill the center of the form. When complete, this formation should resemble a plump mushroom cap. If it lacks proper depth, place the tip of the decorating cone down into the center of the swirl and fill it with icing until it is sufficiently expanded. This bubble will be less smooth than many of the formations in the previous exercises, and will almost always require additional smoothing.

SHAPING AND SMOOTHING SOMETIMES NEED A HAND

Most figures require a certain amount of shaping and smoothing with a palette knife, paint brushes, and a wooden skewer to give them a fine professional finish. Refer to DETAILED DESCRIPTION OF MATERIALS AND EQUIPMENT on page 23 for a complete description of these tools. Their use will require a generous amount of applied practice and experimentation. Each decorator must learn to handle this equipment in a fashion that best achieves the results that he desires.

Hot water is an absolute necessity. Use a hot plate to maintain a pot of nearly boiling water for smoothing each figure. The palette knife, brushes and skewer should be dipped into the water before each use. Moisture prevents icing from sticking to the tools and the heat slightly melts and helps to smooth this high shortening-content icing. Each time one of these tools is dipped into the water, it should be blotted on a damp cloth to remove excess water. It will be necessary for the tools, especially the brushes, to be frequently wiped clean and redipped into the hot water.

LEARN TO USE THE PALETTE KNIFE

The palette knife is generally employed to flatten and to alter contours of a figure, or to smooth extreme irregularities like the rough joints where an arm or leg is intervolved with the body. Use of the palette knife will not be necessary on all figures.

220

LEARN TO USE THE LARGER BRUSHES

The half-inch and one-inch water color brushes are used to smooth broad formations. The student can get along without the one-inch brush for most purposes, but it can be used to an advantage on the larger heads and bodies to make smoothing faster. Neither of these flat brushes is used much for shaping, but mostly to soften harsh lines that are left by the palette knife and to eliminate ripples and bulges that result from uneven pressure. The brush should be held lightly so that its soft bristles are pulled gently along the contours of the buttercream form. Nice long strokes are best; shorter strokes sometimes leave unwanted marks and depressions.

LEARN TO USE THE WOODEN SKEWER

The wooden skewer is used as a stylus to sculpture grooves and hollows. Generally it is used for facial details like the openings for the eyes and the mouth. For sharp cuts like these, the skewer should be held firmly between the thumb and forefinger in much the same way that one holds a pencil.

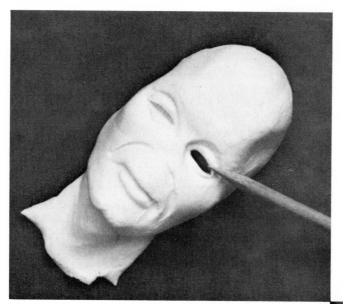

For slighter depressions like the lines around the mouth and eyelids, the skewer should be manipulated gently in a more horizontal position. This allows the sides of its beveled tip to shape rather than to cut into the icing. The decorator may achieve even greater results by spinning the skewer between the thumb and fingers as he etches and shapes the buttercream.

LEARN TO USE THE SMALLER BRUSHES

The Number 6 water color brush will smooth the smaller contoured surfaces like those about the face. It will be used to modify the harsh lines created by the skewer and to produce the ridges and hollows that define the more prominent muscles and bone structures of the face and body.

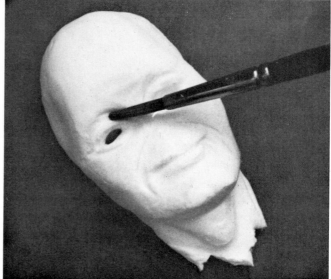

The Number 0 water color brush, like the skewer, is used more as a stylus than as a brush. Its finely pointed bristles are ideal for shaping the corners of a mouth, for defining the tiny margins between the teeth, and for hollowing the nostrils. Its use for smoothing is limited to very small surface areas such as eyes and teeth.

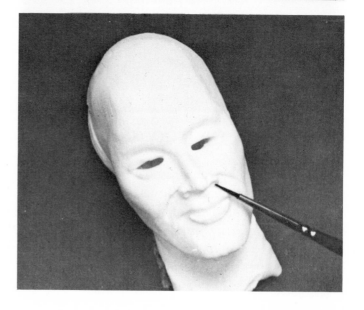

Each decorator should become accustomed to handling the palette knife, skewer, and brushes before he attempts to experiment on completed figures. He will certainly benefit from any time that he spends learning to use these tools. His practice at smoothing some of the basic buttercream formations such as the swirl bubbles and the reversed teardrops will provide him with excellent experience.

Once the student has patiently practiced these exercises and can repeatedly pipe each formation so that he is satisfied with the smoothness and accuracy of each shape, he is ready to proceed with figure piping. Many decorators find figure piping to be much easier than is drawing with pencil and paper. Either one requires a thorough understanding of proportions and balance. Pencil sketches, however, rely heavily on shading to give them a sense of shape and dimension; whereas, icing figures are highlighted by a light source in the room, and natural shadows are cast as the bodies and figures take on life-like depth. With every figure the decorator can feel the incomparable sense of creation. Probably the ultimate satisfaction in figure piping comes with the exhilarating experience of sculpturing a three-dimensional portrait. To create a physiognomy in the image of a person is almost a feeling of producing life itself.

COMIC FIGURES

Comic figures are simplest of all to pipe. They provide great experience for the novice, and the cakes that these little "critters" adorn appeal to nearly everyone. They are more easily translated into bubbles and other elementary forms than are their realistic counterparts. The following comic figures are produced from shapes similar to those in the foregone exercises and each is pictured according to the step-by-step order of production. The first is a jolly elephant that makes use of the tapered "S" formation for its trunk, and the reversed teardrop for its body. The reader will undoubtedly recognize other familiar components in this collection of comic characters.

Plain white buttercream will suffice for practicing the figures that follow. It will not be necessary for the student to mix special colors for any of the figures until he has learned to pipe them with smooth accuracy. This will reduce the probability of wasting both time and materials.

COMIC ELEPHANT

A chubby elephant will fill the bill for children's parties, or for the celebration of a twenty-first birthday. It need not be extremely detailed, so it can be piped quite rapidly, making it a productive but an extra-special decoration.

Fill a parchment cone with icing and cut the tip to at least a quarter-inch opening. Begin with the front of the trunk, and pipe a tapered "S"-curved column that gradually increases to several times its original size. On the finish of the "S" stroke, maintain the pressure and move the tip in a clockwise swirl to form the head; if extra bulk needs to be added so as to improve its shaping, place the tip into the center of the bubble and inflate it with a force of pressure. Indicate the mouth by piping a lower lip below where the trunk merges with the head. Push the tip of the cone into the face near the corner of the mouth to start a cheek bubble. Pull it to a teardrop shape across the base of the head while keeping the tip of the cone slightly depressed into the head form.

Begin below the center of the head to form the curving, reversed teardrop body in one smooth stroke. As the pressure is being increased, gradually raise the tip from the work surface so as to allow the form to expand without rupturing.

Add stubby legs and a tail and smooth the figure with the half-inch water color brush. If some portions of the figure, such as the face or the intersection where the legs join the body, are particularly rough, save some time by first smoothing such areas with a palette knife. Then proceed with the final smoothing by using the brush, dampened with nearly boiling water. Use the point of a wooden skewer to hollow the eye sockets. Pipe a curved column of icing to indicate the partly hidden ear, then form the other ear with a flat bubble that is overpiped with an outline to simulate the folded over edge.

The eyebrow and the outer rim of the eye are piped with black icing from a decorating cone cut to a string-sized opening. Use a similar cone of white buttercream to fill in the eye and to form the tusk and toenails. Add a tiny red tongue and say "Hello" to a perky pachyderm. Make him blue or grey and perhaps endow him with circus trimmings for a child's cake. For the "tippler," pipe the elephant from pink icing and give him droopy eyelids to half cover eyes that are gazing upward. Underline the eyes with bright pink or red to make them look bloodshot, and outline champagne bubbles about the cake. A favorite inscription for such a cake is "HATHY BURPDAY!"

225

227

TRICK-'R-TREAT SCARECROW

This delightful goblin is designed from the basic formations in the beginning exercises of figure piping. It will tease and please the hearts of the young and will provide a perfect Halloween centerpiece for any adult party as well.

With this character, proportions are important. Its body is proportionately the same as the human anatomy, but its pumpkin head is greatly exaggerated by comparison to that of a realistic man.

The decorator will need four large cones of buttercream; one each of orange, blue, yellow, and red. Each will have to be cut so that the opening in the tip is at least equal to the diameter of a pencil. Two smaller cones filled with black and yellow buttercream will be required to complete the facial details. They should each be cut to a string-sized opening. Finally, it will be necessary to fit a cone with a Number 16 star tip for the straw-colored icing. For the proper effect, stripe the inside of the cone with brown, orange and white buttercream before filling it with golden yellow.

The pumpkin is begun with two opposing "C" formations, made with the large cone of orange buttercream. Then the space between them must be filled with a swirl bubble to provide a foundation for the other segments that will complete the head. These remaining segments are columns of buttercream that are tapered at each end. They are piped in *curving*, vertical lines over the foundation. Begin each of these columns with light pressure, gradually increasing the force to plump the column at the midway point. From then on, slowly reduce the pressure to complete the formation.

Use the cone of blue icing to pipe a large reversed teardrop for the body. Add a tapered column for each leg, and overpipe the base of the pant-legs to represent the cuffs.

With the large cone of yellow icing, nearly cover the upper body with two flat, tapered columns, one for each side of the coat. Form the lines at each side, below the head, for the collar and outline the coat front and the ends of the sleeves. The hat is a bubble of red buttercream piped over a circular brim.

Add small black outlines for the eyes, nose, and mouth, and pipe little flat bubbles on the coat for buttons. Use the small cone of yellow icing to fill in the outlined features with highlights, and complete the eyes with black dots for pupils.

The straw sprigs, made with the star tip, should fan out from the center of the opening in the sleeves and pant-legs. Each tuft of straw should be piped in a graceful line. Add straw stuffing so that it appears to be hanging out from the coat, then pull some little wisps of straw-hair from under the brim of the hat.

230

COMIC COWBOY

This cowboy is a perfect example of a comic "people" figure that can be piped swiftly and easily, and it makes use of the same simple formations as does the elephant or the scarecrow.

For this little hombre, prepare one large decorating cone each of flesh tone, brown, grey, and blue. Cut the tip of that decorating cone which is filled with brown buttercream to the diameter of a milkshake straw. The tips of the other cones should be clipped to form half-inch openings. Prepare one other large cone with a Number 16 star tip, and fill it with brown buttercream for the hair.

In addition to the larger cones, the job will require four small parchment cones; one each, of flesh, black, white, and red. Cut the tips of these cones to string-size openings—use these for the smaller details of the figure.

With the large cone of flesh buttercream, pipe a big (about one and one-half inches in diameter) bubble for the head. Make a reversed teardrop body; start with blue, then interrupt the pressure at the cowboy's waistline, and change colors to complete the teardrop formation with grey buttercream. This procedure will dress the upper torso with a blue shirt, and will begin the top portion of his pants.

Use the grey icing to pipe two columns for the legs; cut the pressure to terminate the legs at a point just below the knees, to make room for the boots. This little dude's boots and vest are of brown icing—follow the example in the illustration. Complete the figure with blue columns that are appropriately angled to represent his arms.

Add sprigs of brown hair with the star-tipped decorating cone before piping the cowboy hat. This versatile character can be outfitted and may be detailed with any sort of expression that is deemed appropriate or desirable. Be sure to pipe the figure and its details in the correct proportions and make certain that his body is properly balanced.

The remainder of this lesson on comic figures contains several full-page color photographs of finished cakes. It also includes examples of other simple figures that use, basically, the same techniques that were applied to produce the elephant, the scarecrow, and the cowboy.

Analyze each of the other comic characters. Observe each body segment, and compare it to the basic formation at the beginning of this lesson; then, use the same procedures as were demonstrated in the previous step-by-step photographs to pipe other similar figures.

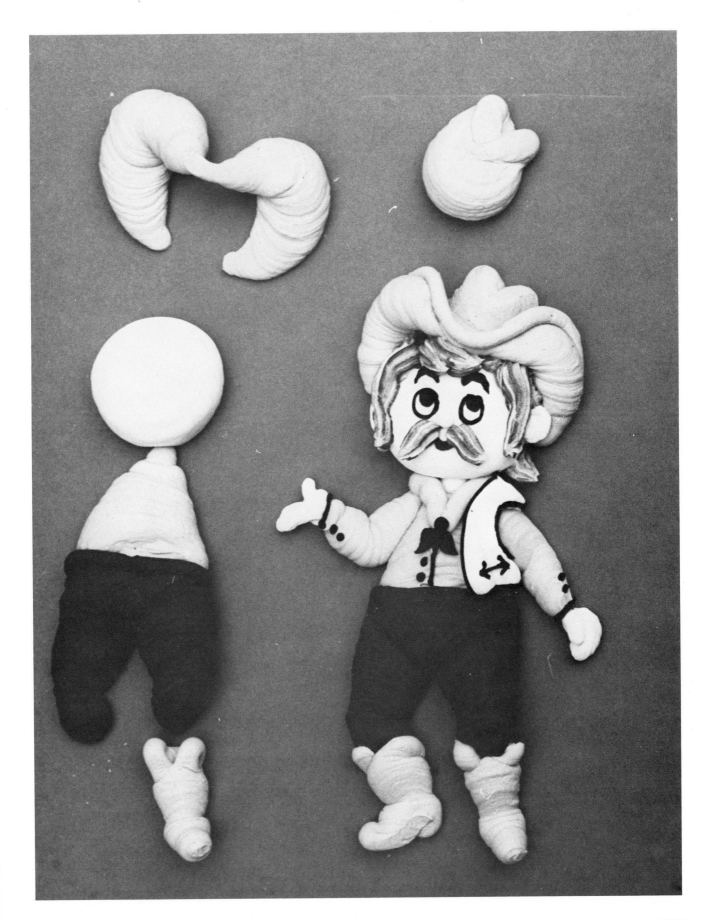

FIGURE PIPING AND THE HUMAN ANATOMY

A decorator can effectively develop his skill for piping the human anatomy with plain white icing. It will not be necessary for the student to use flesh-toned icing until he can confidently produce well-shaped, accurately proportioned figures.

Flesh tones are a mixture of pink, yellow, and brown—natural skin colors range from peach-beige to dark brown. One must begin with approximately equal amounts of pink and yellow; then he should add brown in whatever quantity as may be necessary to produce the desired tone. Skin colors, particularly the deeper tones, will sometimes have a tendency to darken after they are brushed with hot water. The decorator should take this into consideration whenever he mixes the buttercream for his human figures.

Realistic human figures are far more complex than comic buttercream characters. Components of the human anatomy are not merely simple formations, but are precisely controlled shapes that clearly resemble each portion of the body. The experience that the decorator has gained through piping the earlier formations and figures will now prove to be most beneficial.

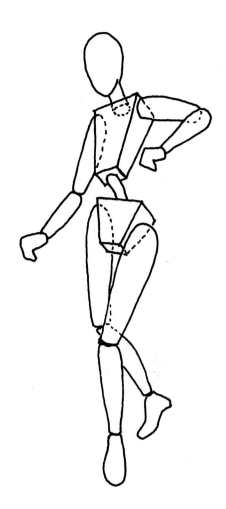

It is highly important that the student must remember the shapes and proportions of the face and body, and it would, therefore, be advisable for him to review the studies on anatomy. When piping the human figure, the formation that was once described as a thick and thin column must now look like an arm or a leg and the bubble must be modified in the image of a head. Pefection of these buttercream translations can only be mastered with repeated trial and effort; by no means, should the student allow himself to be discouraged by his first attempts. There is no easy way to master this creative task. It will take time and practice and then it will take more time and more practice, but the eventual results will be a treasure of naturalistic figures that will truly be a source of satisfaction and pride.

LEARN TO PIPE THE HEAD

The head and face are more easily treated apart from the total body, since many complicated details are associated only with the features of the face. Initially, the student should limit his efforts solely to learning to pipe the head formation. When he has perfected this form to the degree that his attempts consistently render head shapes like those in the illustration, he may proceed to smoothing and to sculpturing features.

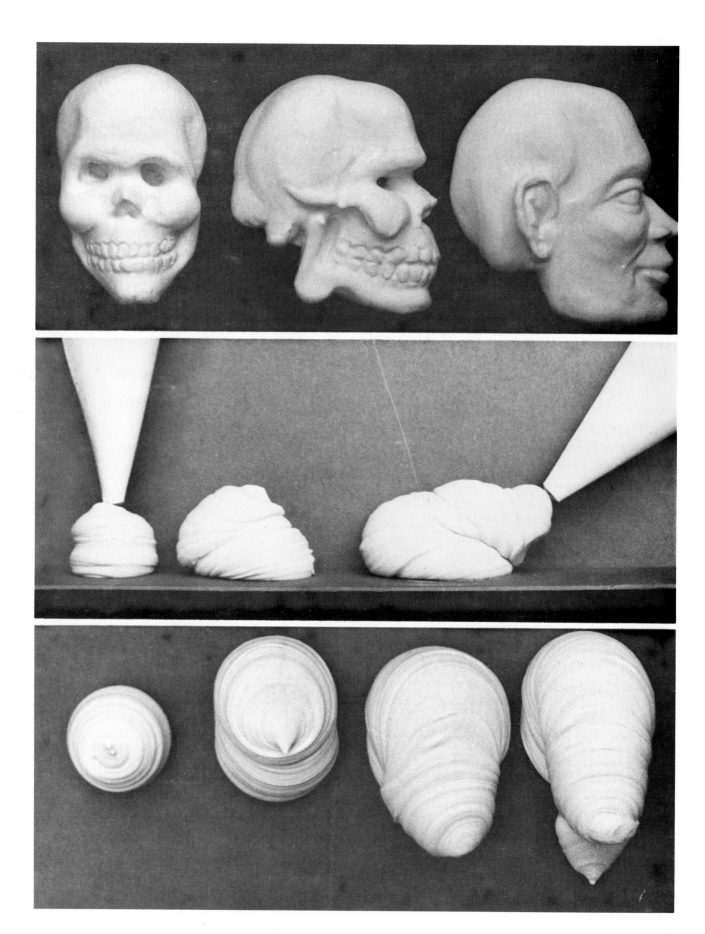

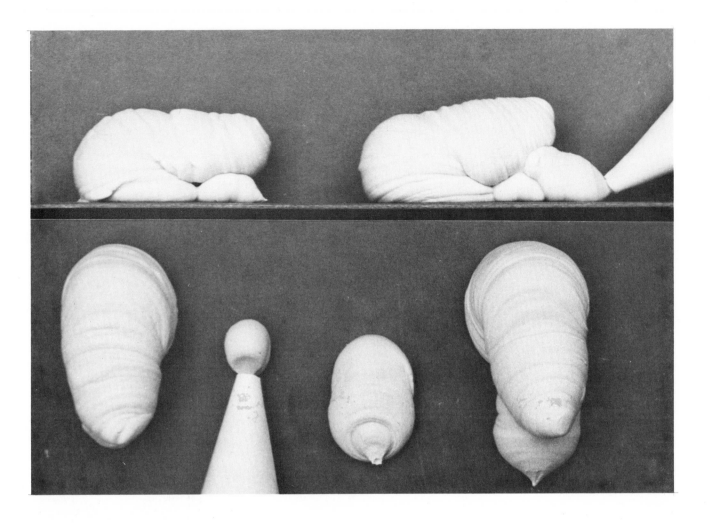

The shape of the buttercream head, when it is viewed from the side, closely resembles the profile of a human skull. The back sphere of the skull is formed by a standing column of icing that acts as a support to balance the oval face. From the beginning of the foundation, the pressure must remain constant throughout the formation of the head, except at the last moment when it is relaxed to form the tapered chin.

The columnar foundation is begun with the same technique that is employed to begin a bubble formation, however, the pressure should be sustained all the while that the decorating cone is being raised. When the column reaches a height comparable to its width, the cone should still be allowed to rise slowly as it is shifted to gently push the top of the column slightly away from the decorator to shape the top of the skull and forehead. With continued pressure to sustain the formation's width, the cone should now be moved in a level line toward the decorator to create an oval column as wide as the foundation, to complete the face. The oval face should rest on top of the foundation in such a way that the lower jaw and chin appear to be suspended without support.

The neck is another column of icing that originates from beneath the jaw. For this, the decorating cone must be angled so that its tip can be inserted up into the underside of the oval face, where the jaw meets the back sphere of the skull.

When, after much practice, the decorator is able to pipe accurately shaped heads time after time, he is ready to create the face. He must now smooth and sculpture the head, and must pipe the nose, ears, and other detailed features.

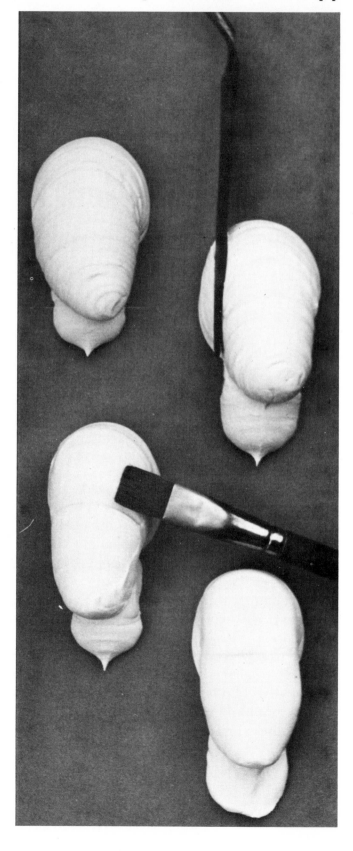

Begin with a head that is piped with a freshly filled cone of white icing. Before filling the cone, remember to stir the icing to rid it of excessive air pockets. The oval head will probably bulge some at the sides of the face. The sides of a person's head, from the lower part of his jaws up to a position above his temples, form nearly straight lines. Therefore, the sides of the buttercream head should be carefully straightened with the moist, clean blade of a palette knife. Take care not to allow the blade to dig into the icing, but merely to shape it. The head is ready to be brushed smooth. Dip the half-inch brush into hot water and blot it lightly on a damp cloth. Gently stroke the form, and if the bristles tend to pull the icing after a few strokes, wipe the brush clean and moisten it again.

When the head has been adequately smoothed, use the point of a skewer to mark the positions for the eyes. Remember to center them halfway between the top of the head and the base of the chin. Dampen the skewer in hot water and, while holding it in a vertical position, gouge out two small openings for the eye sockets. While doing this, twirl the skewer to prevent it from pulling the icing.

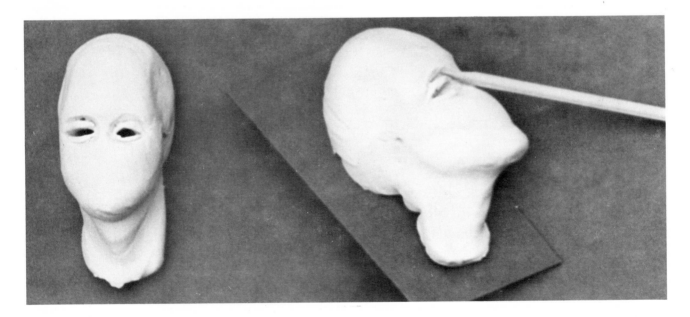

Slant the skewer to gently etch a line above the eyes to form the contoured eyelids and to define the brow line. This will tend more to shape the area, rather than actually to remove any of the icing. The lower eyelid and the upper plane of the cheek should be shaped with a lighter touch so that the cheek is only slightly beveled.

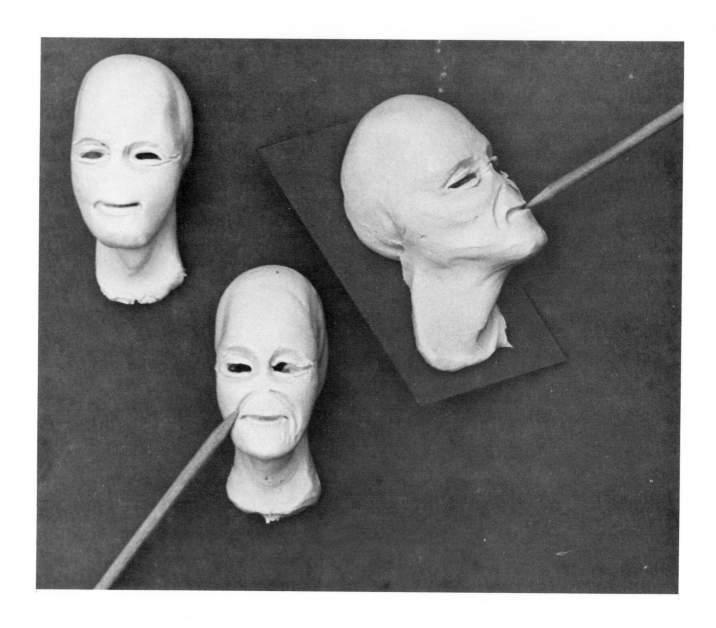

Hold the wooden skewer vertically to carve the mouth opening. If necessary, refer to the guide lines in the instructions for drawing the face in its proper proportions. Turn the mouth line slightly upward at each side for a natural expression.

After the mouth has been shaped, scratch a tiny mark on the face to indicate the position for the tip of the nose. Then, hold the skewer horizontally to form the depressions for the smile lines that extend diagonally from either side of the nose to just beyond the corners of the mouth. Another slight depression should be made on the lower lip at each corner of the mouth to lend the realistic contours.

Use a decorating cone with a small string-sized opening to pipe a line to accentuate the lower lip. If, at this time, the upper region between the mouth and the nose seems unnaturally shallow, use the same decorating cone to add a layer of icing. This added formation should be smoothed with the Number 6 water color brush. At this point, it may be necessary to re-emphasize the smile lines.

246

Accentuate the upward curves of the mouth to change the more sober expression to a happy smile. To convey an air of displeasure or sadness, angle the corners of the mouth downward. To make the face reflect the uncontrolled appearance of intoxication, etch the mouth line with one side turned upward, the other curved downward.

Do the rest of the shaping mostly with the Number 6 water color brush. This brush works well for smoothing the harsh lines left by the skewer. Make the brush follow the contours to shape and to smooth the areas according to the way the finished face should appear. Each student will employ different techniques that best fit the situation, and there are no real set rules except to be gentle and to learn to be precise. See that the brush is under careful control at all times so that no more icing is eliminated or depressed than should be. Be certain to keep the brush moist with hot water and wiped free of any excess icing.

For the delicate and sharper details such as the corners of the mouth and eye openings, use the Number 0 water color brush. It can be dipped into the hot water and formed to a fine point between the thumb and forefinger. This same technique can be used on the Number 6 brush either to shape it to a point or to flatten its bristles, to fit the contours of the figure.

After the face is satisfactorily smoothed and shaped, it is ready to receive the nose, ears, and other details. The directions that follow for piping the nose and ears, will be more easily understood if the student will first practice the formations before he attempts to apply them to the buttercream heads.

247

LEARN TO PIPE THE NOSE

The size of the nose will depend, of course, on the size of the head. The noses, for the smaller figures that will most often be used, will be made with a parchment cone cut to a string-sized opening. The formations in this illustration are purposely made larger for easier comprehension. The student also may conduct his practice with a large cone, but should still become familiar with the results that can be expected from a smaller cone.

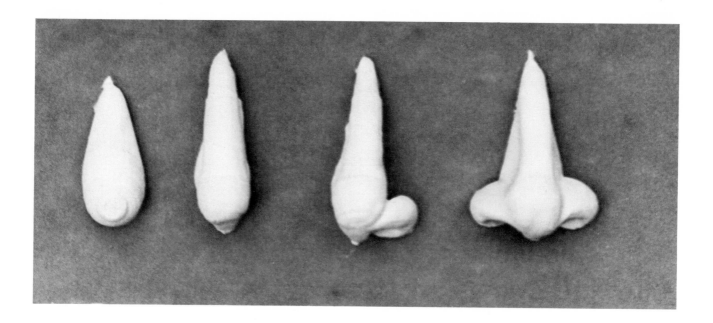

The main portion of the nose is basically a reversed teardrop formation. In order that it may be piped with realistic depth, it should be formed over a reversed teardrop foundation. This foundation should be piped in the position that will be occupied by the lower half of the nose. Build the tapered foundation and overpipe it with whatever shape most closely resembles the nose style that fits the proposed character of the face. As the pressure is relaxed to form the lower end of the nose, move the cone downward to produce a line of icing to simulate the strip of cartilage that separates the nostrils.

To add more natural width, insert the tip of the decorating cone into the side of the nose, close to the surface of the face, just above the position where the nostril begins to flare. Apply a small amount of pressure and move the tip of the decorating cone down toward the base of the nose. Then permit the form to swell briefly just while raising the cone to produce the tapered outline of the nostril. Repeat the same process to complete the other side of the nose.

On larger portraits it is often necessary to add a little extra icing where each side of the nose blends into the muscle that forms the cheek. This can be accomplished by inserting the tip of the cone into the side of the nose so that, with gentle pressure, both forms will merge into a single smooth contour.

248

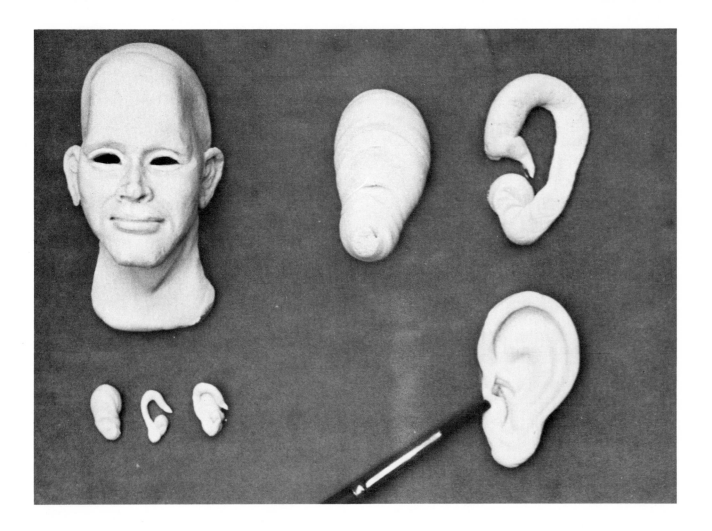

LEARN TO PIPE THE EARS

Ears for a small figure are made with a parchment cone cut to a string-sized opening at the tip, and they need relatively little detail. On larger portraits, some attention must be given to the inner contours; however, the ears, unlike the other facial features, do not play much of a role in whether or not one person recognizes another. Therefore, the important thing to remember is that each formation should look like "any ear."

Begin with two bubble foundations, one piped on each side of the head. Remember that the tops of the ears should be on a line level with the eyebrows, and the bottoms should be level with the tip of the nose.

This foundation is formed with the same technique as was the swirl bubble. Instead of being round, the ear is more nearly like a lopsided oval (see the illustration).

Pipe the foundation, then, beginning midway down on the edge of the oval where it fastens to the head, use the decorating cone to form a small bubble of icing. This little bubble will simulate the tab of flesh that protects the opening to the ear canal. Move the cone upward, higher on the oval and apply enough pressure to begin a band of icing that will encircle the outer rim of the ear. To accent the "lobe," retrace the bottom of the ear.

For larger portraits, the details inside the ear are a formation of ridges that are piped and smoothed with a brush before the outer rim is added.

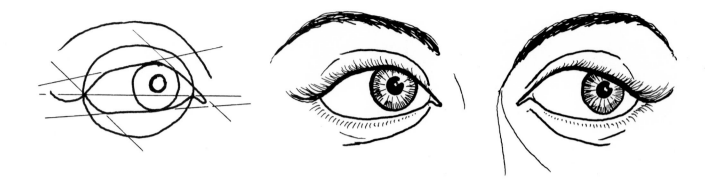

LEARN TO PIPE THE EYES

The above illustration is submitted as a guide for determining the realistic shapes of the eyelids and of the structure of the eyes. The eye sockets will probably require some reshaping in preparation to receive the detailed formation of the eyes.

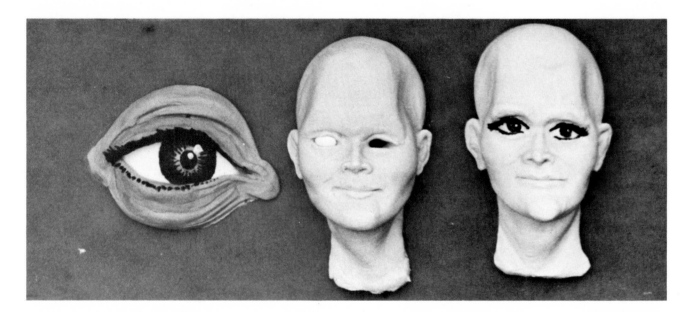

Use flesh-colored buttercream in a small parchment cone and cut the tip to a string-sized opening. Accentuate the upper and lower eyelids, following the shapes suggested by the lines in the illustration. Smooth these additional icing formations with the moistened Number 6 water color brush to blend them into the surrounding contours.

Cut the point of a small cone of white buttercream to form a large string-sized opening. Insert the tip of the cone inside the hollow eye sockets and, with moderate pressure, fashion a smooth, oval bubble of icing for the eyeball. The "iris" (colored portion of the eye) is piped with a cone of any desirable color with a fine-cut opening. For small figures, the iris can appropriately be piped from a single medium tone. However, to simulate a more realistic eye for larger portraits, the iris color should be piped in a lighter tone near the center and then outlined with a darker shade of the same hue.

A black dot will provide the pupil for the eye. Add a small speck of white buttercream at the same proximity in the iris of each eye, to provide a natural looking highlight and to add a realistic reflection which will lend a sparkle of life to the eye.

To pipe the eyelashes, the decorator should use dark-colored buttercream (either black or brown) in a cone with its tip cut to a very fine string opening. Each eyelash is a tiny, individual hair, and can best be imitated with a fine thread of icing which is pulled straight out from the upper lid. One must begin at the outer corner of the eye and should pipe a series of lashes so that each stands independently, aimed diagonally from the position of the nose, to form a line across the edge of the upper eyelid.

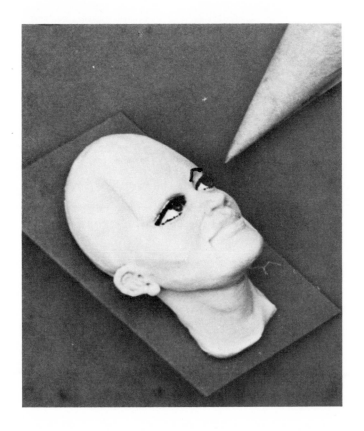

Eyebrows will complete the expressive eyes. On smaller figures, a thin graceful line will suffice for each eyebrow on the female face, and a broader, more bushy line will be appropriate for the masculine brow. The eyebrows on a large portrait must be composed of individual hairs that are made with a small decorating cone like that which was used for the eyelashes. Coloration for the brows can range from hues that match the figure's hair color, to darker tones of that color.

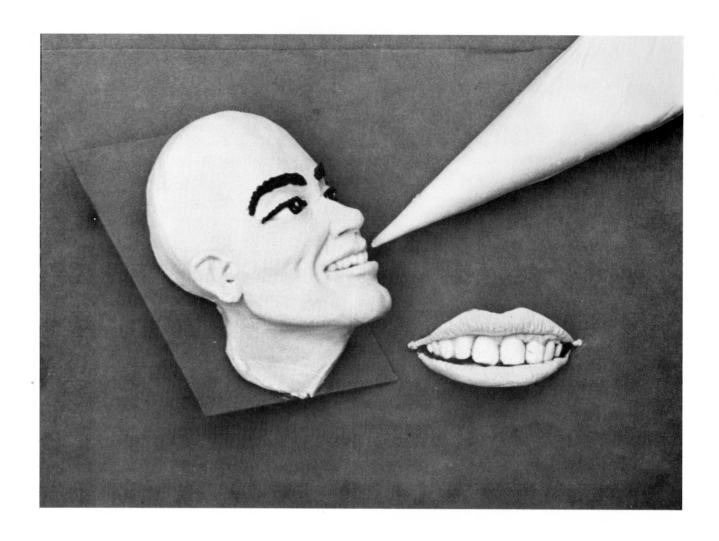

LEARN TO FORM TEETH AND OTHER DETAILS OF THE MOUTH

For large portraits, and for even smaller faces that are extremely detailed, one can pipe teeth with a small cone of white buttercream. Each tooth should be piped individually, beginning with those that are barely visible in the back of the jaw, and working toward the front of the mouth. Final shaping of each tooth should be done with the Number 0 water color brush. This operation requires a skilled, steady hand and a keen observation of the shapes of real teeth.

The lips should receive their final shaping with either the Number 0 or the Number 6 water color brush. The lower lip should be smoothed with a very light touch so that it will remain full and rounded. The upper lip must be beveled—the side of the brush's bristles can be used to push against the icing so as to flatten the edge of the lip into a realistic shape. When the mouth is completed, the decorator should paint the lips and cheeks of female figures with pink liquid food color diluted with water. Small male faces look best without this extra coloring, however the lips on larger male portraits can and should be tinted with a soft tone of diluted pink combined with a touch of brown.

HAIR STYLES

In an earlier portion of this chapter which was devoted to the study of anatomy, it was pointed out that hair styles play an important role in any artistic caricature. The best method for the student to learn how to form contemporary hair styles is for him first to observe live people and to study pictures of models in magazines and catalogs, and then to practice imitating various coiffures with buttercream.

The decorator should not attempt to add the hair, particularly if it is a long style, until the figure is fully clothed. This rule applies, as well, to portraits that have any sort of garment around the neck or shoulders. Also, if the figures are nude or are scantily clad, one should shape and smooth the body to completion before adding the hair.

The texture for semi-straight or for wavy hair styles can most realistically be reproduced with a decorating cone that is fitted with either a Number 14 or a Number 16 star tip. With a long graceful stroke, the decorator should pipe each lock so that it emanates from the top of the head at the position where the hair is parted. For shorter hair, styled with small curls, one should begin with a row at the base of the head and should layer the curls, one row above the other until he reaches the part.

On portraits where the necessity of very fine detail is indicated, the decorator can pipe individual strands of hair from a small cone that is cut to produce an extremely fine string. This same sort of cone works excellently for producing any type of hair style that seems to be composed of individual strands that are tightly curled. These tightly curled strands can be simulated if the decorator holds the decorating cone out from the surface of the head and applies very strong pressure. One must move the cone in a tight circular pattern, constantly shifting positions until the desired area is completely covered. The decorator should continue the pattern with sustained pressure to complete the hair style to its proper depth.

If the portrait is of a man, the sideburns should be piped in advance of the hair style. Light sideburns can be indicated with the small plain-cut cone, but if a bushier appearance is desired, the student may experiment with a small star tip. This same metal tip will provide the ideal texture for a moustache or beard—for either, one must work from the center of the face outward to the sides.

254

LEARN TO PIPE THE BODY

A decorator should have such a thorough understanding of anatomy that he can visualize how the finished subject should look before he begins to pipe the buttercream figure. As he assaults the cake's smooth surface, the artist must combine an assortment of bubbles and tubular formations. He must force extra pressure here, then execute just the right curve there until finally the buttercream form, with a small amount of brushing and shaping, will become that figure which once was only traced in the decorator's imagination.

The student's sensitivity and his ability to perform these figure piping skills can be acquired only through his practice of drawing the muscles and the skeletal structure and by his careful observation of people.

The decorator, when he is piping the total human figure, must take into account its height and the amount of space available on the work surface.

Use the same procedure that was employed for drawing the human figure with pencil and paper. Prepare the work surface by piping two dots of icing to indicate the height of the figure—these two dots should be adjacent to the proposed placement of the top of the head and the bottom of the heels. Draw horizontal lines to divide the distance between the dots into eight equal segments and use this scale as a guide for practicing to pipe the buttercream body.

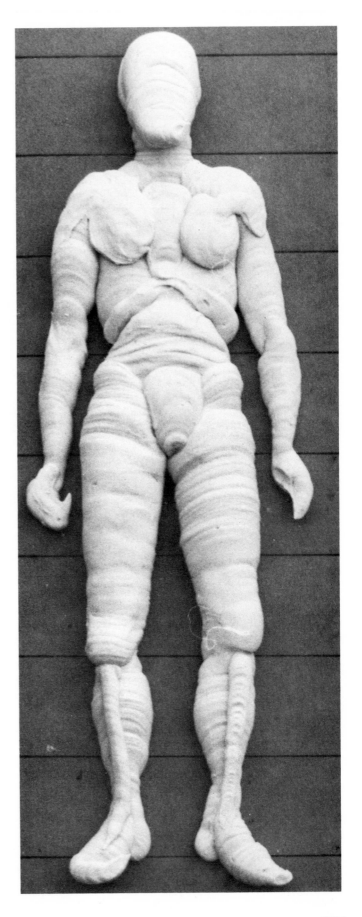

Pipe the head and neck in the same manner as was suggested in the earlier exercise but confine the oval formation within the space adjacent to the top segment of the scale.

Extend two lines from the sides of the neck; start them about a quarter-segment below the chin line and angle them downward to the positions for the shoulder joints. This will be the shoulder line at the top of the trunk.

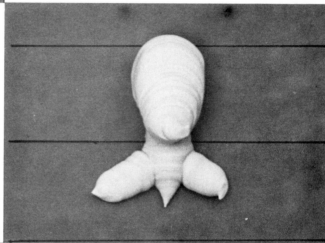

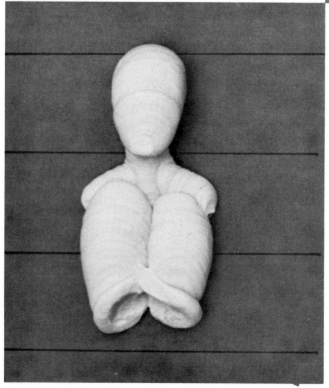

The rib cage is formed of two columns of buttercream, each like a long, oval bubble. Begin at the shoulder line, and use firm pressure to produce a full, well-rounded column; however, begin to relax the pressure about midway down so that the formation will be narrower at its base. Cut the pressure and allow the tip of the cone to descend to the work surface; then, increase the pressure to overpipe the base of the column with a curved line to simulate the bottom rib—this line should extend from the back, around the outer edge and across the front of the rib cage, to the position at the base of the breastbone (see the skeleton on page 198).

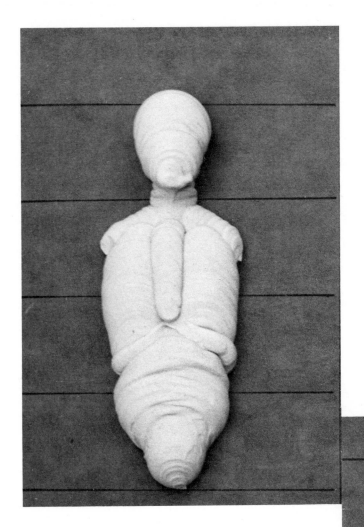

Pipe a flat column of icing for the breast-bone to cover the margin between the two segments of the rib cage. Next, form the abdominal or stomach region. Insert the tip of the cone into the lower cavity between each bubble of the rib cage, and draw the cone downward. Increase the pressure until the abdominal cavity, just below the chest, is filled; then, move the tip from side to side enough to expand the bubble to almost the width of the chest. Complete the abdomen by pulling a column of icing downward to the center line of the figure.

Complete the trunk by piping two tear-drops on each side of the column at the base of the abdomen; the teardrops should form a heart shape that is wide, but not pointed at the bottom. These formations should occupy the same general area and shape as does the pelvis in a sketch of the body.

257

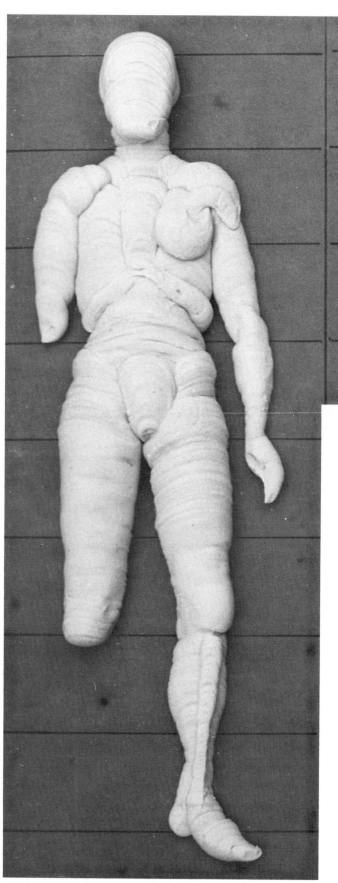

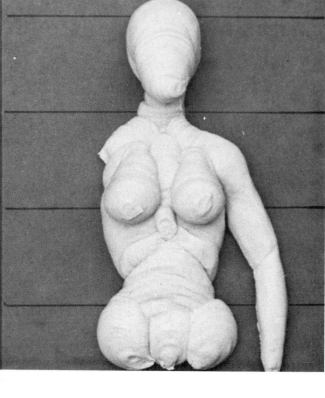

Now the figure is ready to receive the arms and legs. Force the tip of the cone into the shoulder to begin the cylindrical column of icing for the upper arm. Think about the muscle structure of the arm as the decorating cone travels downward, and control the flow of buttercream so that it imitates that form. Discontinue the pressure for a moment at the elbow, enough to force the tip of the decorating cone back into the base of the just completed form, then begin the lower arm—this section of the arm is like a long teardrop. Just below the wrist it should be offset to indicate the shape of the hand.

The detailed fingers can be added either now or after the body is smoothed, but they should be done with a small cone like the one which was used for the nose and ears. This will allow each finger and thumb to be made individually, so as to add greater realism to the figure.

Start the upper leg by inserting the tip of the parchment cone into the side of the pelvis at a position half a segment above the midway line on the scale and begin to pipe a column of icing. Increase the pressure in the upper thigh area, then gradually diminish the force so as to indicate that narrower portion of the leg which is just above the knee. Allow the pressure to swell momentarily to add the small bulge for the kneecap at the base of the upper leg.

Immediately slip the tip of the cone under the kneecap and proceed with that column of buttercream which will form the lower leg. While moving the cone downward, expand the column to indicate the calf muscle; then, let the pressure relax so as to narrow the formation above the ankle, and follow through to the base of the heel. Discontinue the pressure for a moment, gently elevate the decorating cone, then resume just enough pressure to trace a thin column upward over the heel bone, almost to the ankle. Now build a teardrop for the foot—learn to modify this teardrop so that it really looks like a foot.

The main bone in the lower leg is near the surface. To indicate this dominating feature, overpipe the front of the leg with a slightly curved vertical column so that it extends from the kneecap down to the inner side of the ankle. This bead of icing should be formed with the tip of the cone slightly depressed into the lower leg so that the overlay and the original column will almost appear to be a single mass.

Use a small decorating cone with its tip cut to a string-sized opening to complete the foot with small bubbles for the toes. These bubbles should form a diagonal line from the smallest toe, at the outer edge of the foot, forward to the tip of the big toe.

Accent the breast area of either the male or female figure with extra icing. The female breast is like a reversed teardrop. Insert the tip of the large decorating cone into the center of one side of the rib cage, at a position that is level with the armpit. Begin to move the cone downward and gradually increase the pressure so that the base of the teardrop is extended to just below the line at the bottom of the second segment. With the smaller decorating cone, make a tiny bubble just outside the center of each breast to form the nipple.

A man's chest is muscular, thus each breast should be piped with the cone perpendicular to the rib cage, and should be formed with a circular motion like that which was used to form the swirl bubble. Pipe the left breast of the figure with a clockwise motion, the right breast with a counterclockwise motion, and allow the end of the swirl to trail upward toward the shoulder, then to arch across the top of the armpit and to terminate into the muscle of the upper arm.

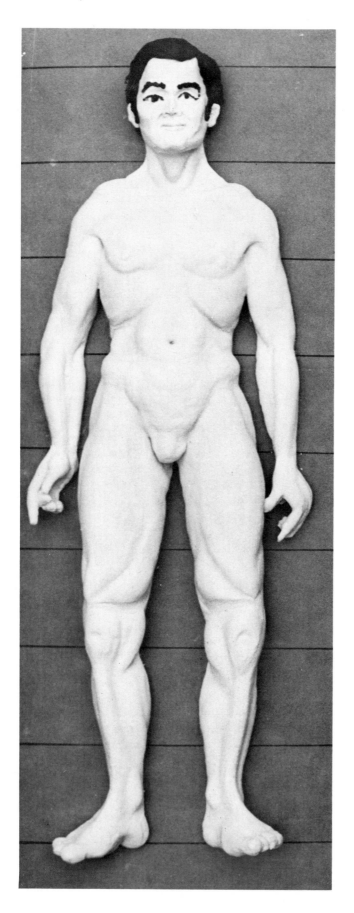

Fill any portions of the body which have not been adequately formed. The figure is now ready to be smoothed with hot water and the brushes. When smoothing the body, try to include depressions in the proper areas and to accent each mass of muscles. Use the half-inch water color brush for the initial smoothing of larger surfaces. Use the Number 6 brush to shape small depressions and to blend any formations where there is not adequate room to use the larger brush. Don't forget to moisten the brushes frequently.

The nude male figure will demand careful attention to the details of the muscle formations—almost as much attention as was necessary to form the precise features of the head and face.

Even after the figure is smoothed, some parts of the structure may need to be emphasized or filled in. To do so, insert the tip of the decorating cone into the body and use sufficient pressure to inflate it with an adequate amount of buttercream. Then use whichever brush seems appropriate to re-smooth that area.

Smoothly contour the female figure. Since her muscles are not so well developed as those of the male, employ gentler pressure when using either of the brushes to shape and to sculpture the female body. Be more concerned with the general shape and contours of her figure rather than with the particular formation of individual muscles.

COMPLETE THE FACIAL DETAILS

Practice several male and female bodies until they can be done with relatively good speed; otherwise, it will be difficult to finish their torsos, arms and legs before the buttercream heads become too well-set to be easily workable. When a buttercream formation dries for too long a time before it is worked, the icing will become porous, will resist plying and it may develop a slight crust that cannot be smoothed, even with hot water. Keep practicing until the bodies can be completed with speed and with relative ease and then attend to the facial details of the heads.

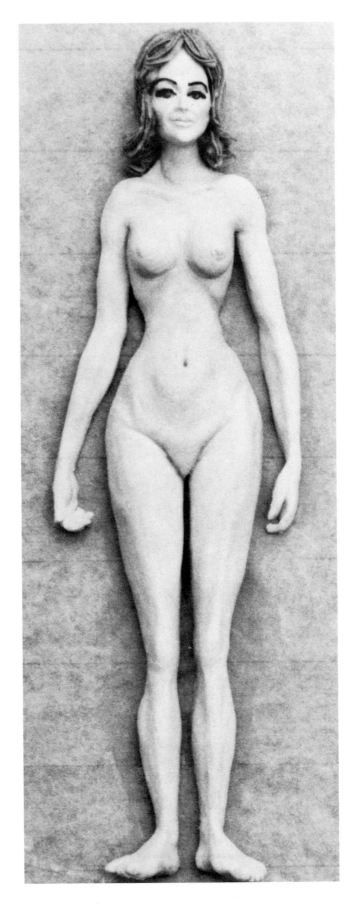

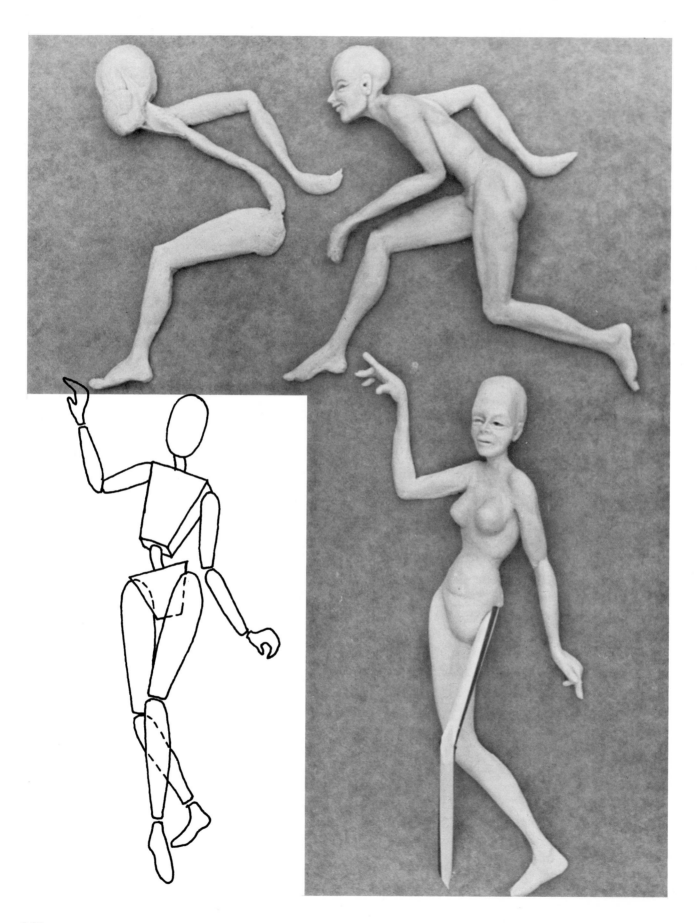

PROFILE POSITION

When the figure is piped in a profile position, the procedure must be altered. Since part of one arm or leg may be obstructed from view by another portion of the body, this member must be piped first. Position the head and neck, then form the line that represents the backbone. Pipe the portion of the arm that will be revealed behind the trunk of the body. The leg on that same side of the body must also be completed before construction of the leg that is closer to the viewer.

Throughout the formation of this type of figure, consider the shape of the body in profile and be aware of its width; then, build the figure with enough depth so that the observer will be comfortable with its dimensions. Make the trunk of the figure slightly more than half-a-body deep, almost as though it were sliced off just beyond the far side of the neck.

THREE-QUARTER POSITION

Often the figure can be made to be more interesting if it is piped in a three-quarter position. This position would be indicated when the figure is turned midway between a straight forward view and a profile view. Follow the same order of procedure as was suggested for the profile position, but allow more of the figure's trunk to show by angling it on a diagonal to the surface of the cake.

That arm or leg which is nearer the observer can be elevated with the support of a plastic drinking straw (the thin bar straw works better). The straw must be bent and the bend must correspond to the knee joint of the leg. That segment of the straw below the bend should be a half-inch longer than the measurement (from the knee to the heel) of the lower leg. The top segment will be longer and will support the upper leg—insert the end of this segment into the cake so that it enters just above the base of the spine. From that point, to the bend, the exposed top segment of the straw should be comparable to the length of the upper leg. To complete the support, insert the extra half-inch of the lower segment into the cake at that position which is to be occupied by the figure's heel.

The straw for the arm should be bent in two places; once at the shoulder joint and once again at the elbow. Leave a long enough section of the straw, above the shoulder joint, so that it can be inserted through the figure and into the cake for support; then, trim off the excessive length. Pipe the arm and leg over the straw foundations to achieve a truly three-dimensional figure.

CLOTHING AND THE HUMAN FIGURE

To this point in figure piping, for a very important reason, this text has dealt only with the undressed human form. The human body has shape, dimensions, and contours; therefore, the student must realize that a garment, when it is placed over a figure, will assume much the same form as does the body itself. In essence, clothing is a covering for the body and it, therefore, must reflect the shape of that form which it covers.

This lesson in clothing the figure is important even to the cartoon style of figure piping, but is absolutely essential if the decorator hopes to pipe truly realistic human figures. In order for the student to comprehend and to master this technique, it will be important for him to make careful observations of different kinds of fabrics. He should be aware of the different varieties of materials and of their weights and textures. Important too, is the observation of how these different fabrics drape or fold, and how this difference is affected by whatever way these fabrics are suspended.

Many fabrics stretch, but few are as elastic as the skin. Articles of clothing, although they basically follow the contours of the body, sometimes wrinkle and fold and bulge in places where the body does not. A loose fitting garment scarcely touches some parts of the body, yet the form beneath is evident. Where does such a garment actually come into contact with a part of the body? How is this situation affected when the body is in motion? How much of the body's shape is visible beneath the garment when no action is involved? If this is a lightweight article of clothing, how differently would it be affected by motion if it were made of heavy fabric? These are questions which the student should ask himself as he makes his observations.

Some of the questions will be answered on the following pages, however, the variables involved are too many. Therefore, this lesson will provide a few ideas, but the reader is encouraged to study the examples which he sees around him every day. Another way for the decorator to conveniently study and to collect excellent examples is for him to clip photographs and drawings from magazines and catalogs or from newspaper advertisements.

It was previously suggested that each reader should prepare a catalog of ideas. A section on costumes could also include a few pages devoted to examples of different kinds of fabrics and, more specifically, to examples of the way those fabrics appear when they are fitted and draped over the human form.

The man's jacket and trousers in the illustration are examples of those heavier fabrics which are used for most coats and suits. The material hangs from the shoulder seam in bulky folds over the arm.

The woman's dress is of thinner, softer fabric, similar to that which is used for most dresses, shirts and blouses. This lighter weight material, where it gathers around the waist and the sleeves, wrinkles in tight folds. Notice too, that the fitted top of her dress clings closely to the shape of her torso, while the full skirt drapes loosely.

When a person is standing relatively still, the weight of the fabric makes it tend to hang straight downward, no matter how the body is positioned. Also, the sleeve of a coat, when the arm is in a horizontal position, hangs freely below the arm. One must keep in mind, when he is drawing or piping such a figure, that the wrist should emerge from the top part of a loose sleeve, not from the center.

Motion has an effect, particularly on lightweight materials. When a figure, wearing a loosely fitted garment, is in motion, the suspended fabric will trail the body. Therefore, when he is piping a running form, the decorator can use this technique so as to emphasize that rushing action.

266

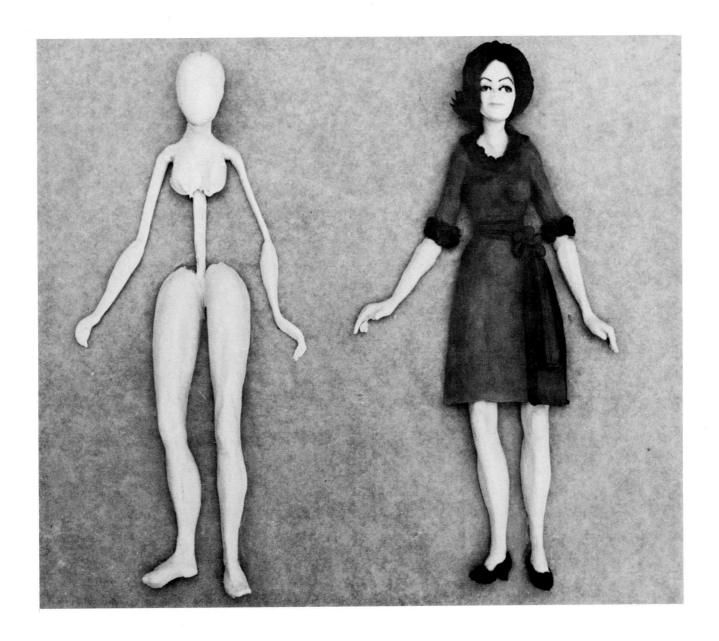

LEARN TO DRESS THE FIGURE

When piping a figure with clothing, begin with the head and neck, and also form any part of the chest area that may show—this will depend on the cut of the garment. If it's a female figure to be adorned with a dress or skirt, pipe a tubular line to represent the position and length of the spine. Then pipe the legs in their proper forms and locations. Add thin lines of icing to depict the positions of the arms and proceed by filling out those portions of each arm which will be exposed. Smooth the figure and shape the face, including all the details except for the hair.

Use the properly colored icing for each part of the garment, and overpipe the related portion of the figure. The garment should take on the form that best represents that portion of the body which it covers, but extra fullness should be allowed according to the surplus of material beyond that amount which is needed to cover the body.

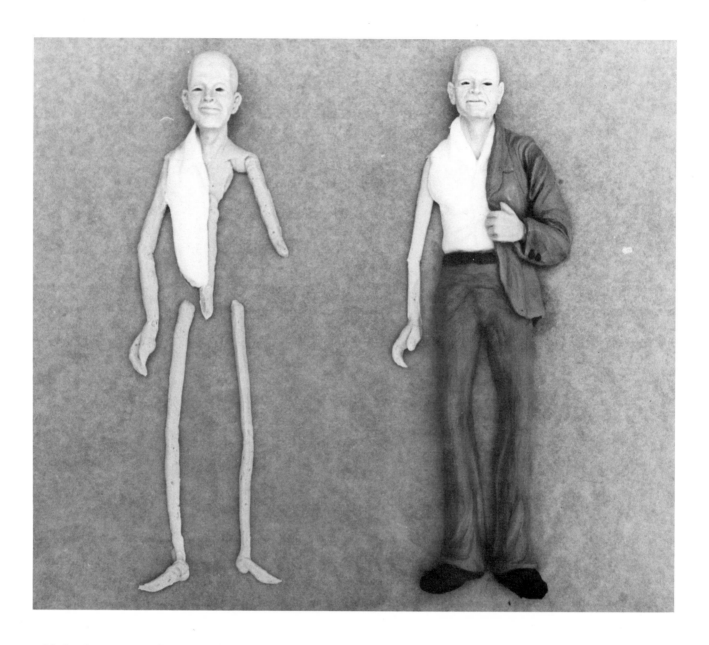

If the figure is to be attired in trousers, begin with the head, the neck, and a line for the arms, like that procedure which was described on the previous page; this time however, pipe the chest area with buttercream of the appropriate color for the shirt or blouse. Next, form the top of the trousers and the trousers' legs in those same shapes and positions which would otherwise be represented and occupied by the lower torso and the legs of a nude figure.

If the figure is wearing a suit, pipe in only that part of the shirt which will be visible beneath the coat. The coat, in this case, will form most of the upper part of the body; the coat's sleeves will provide the shape of the figure's arms. Remember to pipe the coat in that shape which most accurately depicts the weight and texture of its fabric, but also be sure to indicate as much of the body's shape as is necessary to show that the figure is fully formed.

Pipe the hair style and add shoes. Include any other details which will help to reinforce that image which the figure is supposed to convey.

An accent of color, a tiny button, or even a zipper—often, one of these will be that "just right" accessory which makes the character seem to come to life.

268

EFFICIENT, PRODUCTIVE
FIGURE PIPING

To make figure piping more productive, select a few body positions that can be applied again and again to interpret different activities. For instance, the position of the body for a golfer and a baseball player or even for a woodsman wielding an ax will be much the same. A figure in a seated position can be used over and over again to depict many occupations by the simple repositioning of its arms or of the angle of its head or by changing the background setting and the objects in the scene.

Learn to correct mistakes by analyzing them; then start over. Practice, practice, practice! Don't be satisfied with a mediocre likeness. It is not enough to perfect the head and facial features, only to complete the figure with an unbalanced, poorly proportioned body. Practice will not only develop accuracy but will also help to improve the speed that is necessary for efficient production.

Take pride in developing a real work of art. The reward is in doing one's level best. The results of perfecting these figures will be rewarding indeed, and will give the student a tremendous sense of satisfaction. Don't forget the importance and the value of learning to work in a speedy and productive manner. As certainly as "haste makes waste," so does slowness make waste when it is a result of lack of practice and of underdeveloped skill. To endure patiently the basic practice efforts, and to perfect those fundamental skills which are vital to the creation of productive, artistically accurate figures, should be "the goal." Figure piping will then be fun and will be a profitable pursuit.

270

272

LEARN TO PIPE REALISTIC ANIMALS

To this point, this text has dealt with figures that could be arranged into specific categories; each example has been composed of common, basic formations. The comic figures, in a broad general sense, take their origin from the set of primary shapes that were adapted to buttercream formations for the purpose of training the decorator in speed, pressure, wrist action, and in the discipline of control. Human figures, although they are affected by the details of individual characteristics, are each produced from a rudimentary configuration.

Now the decorator must deal with an extensive spectrum of shapes, for "ANIMAL" is a broad category. Each type of animal has an explicit design that has to be subjected to careful analysis, then to be sketched so that the decorator will become familiar with the composition of its body. Finally, the concept must be transformed into a three-dimensional icing figure.

No longer can the decorator pipe simple bubbles for the head and body as was previously done with the comic figures. He must think of definite shapes, and should construct each portion of the animal's body to conform with those shapes, both in structure and in relative position to the other parts of the figure. The most important factors involved in recreating a specific subject are structure, balance, and proportion. Once the student has studied the text, he should sketch, then practice with buttercream.

With this vast world so fully inhabited with all manner of creatures, an attempt to show detailed explanations of how to create buttercream likenesses of a wide variety of animals was impossible. The approach which seemed most reasonable, therefore, was for this author to show examples of a few of the familiar and most frequently asked-for types.

The examples that follow, providing that the reader practices and strives to faithfully reproduce each of them, should impart adequate experience to the student and should enable him to use that same training as a guide for piping other animals.

Generally, realistic animals will have to be piped in a semi-crude form so as to produce their initial shape and bulk. Refinements will have to be made with the palette knife.

Even though the decorator will be concerned only with one view of the animal, he must consider how the subject would look if it were observed from different angles in order for him to sculpture realistic bulk and contours. Most of the smoothing, after the artist completes the shaping with the palette knife, will be performed with the half-inch water color brush.

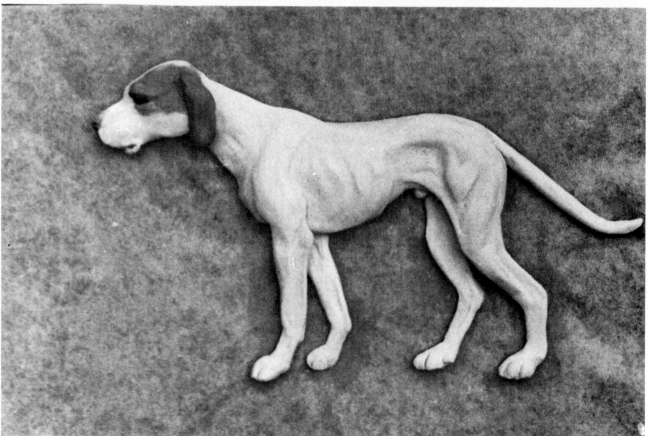

274

CHAPTER VI

Ice Cream Cone Figurines and Cake Sculpturing Fundamentals

Assemble Ice Cream Cone Frameworks
Miniature Figurines
Cake Sculpturing Fundamentals

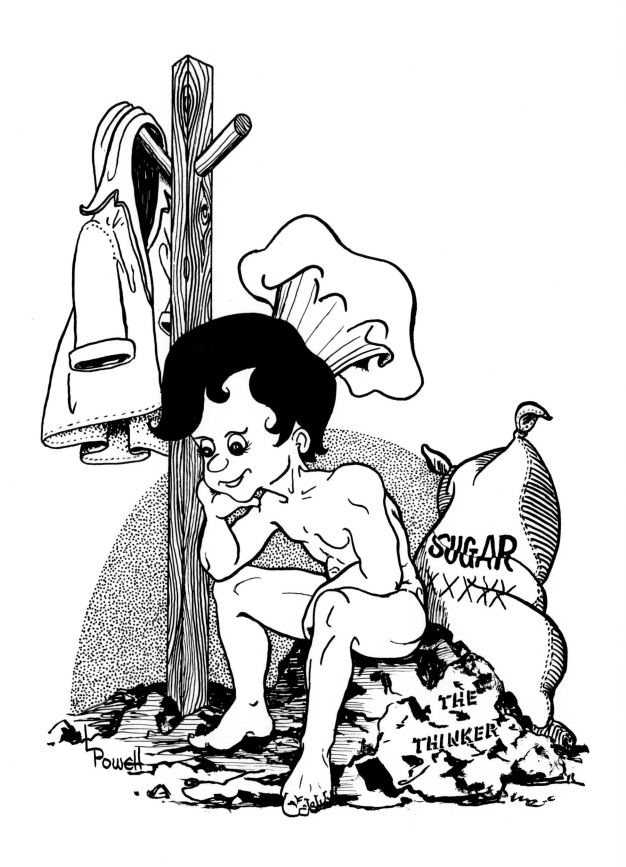

Ice Cream Cone Figurines and Cake Sculpturing Fundamentals

Ice cream cone figurines are miniature stand-up sculptures which are created with buttercream over a specially assembled ice cream cone foundation. These statuettes can be made in the images of dolls, angels, witches, owls, and of many animals. They are more versatile than are the three-dimensional figures that are piped directly on the cake, in the respect that they can be produced ahead of time and may be placed on a cake just moments before the order is to be claimed by the customer. Pre-sculptured figures of this type provide a quick solution to the last minute request of a walk-in shopper who wants something special.

Angels, santas, witches, and owls are easy to make and they add variety to the special holiday ideas. One should not underestimate the value of having extras of these special decorations on hand during the rush periods. If he has any spare time available, the decorator can mass produce several figures of one kind so that he doesn't have to fill new decorating cones for each individual figurine.

An angel can be transformed into a charming bride by the replacement of her halo and wings with a simple veil of gathered lace. One can add a bouquet of tiny buttercream blossoms with colors coordinated to match an arrangement of flowers on the cake; this would make a lovely table centerpiece to delight the hostess of any bridal shower. Owls, because of their popularity as collector's items, are in year 'round demand, but are especially apt for Halloween and for the graduation season.

SUPPORTING FRAMEWORK

The foundation for each mini-sculpture is made from parts of two pointed ice cream cones, assembled with buttercream, reinforced with a plastic drinking straw and supported on a four-inch square of cardboard.

MAKE PREPARATIONS FOR ASSEMBLY

The ice cream cones for the framework of each mini-sculpture are bonded together with buttercream. The buttercream provides adhesive and also enough weight to prevent the figure from tipping over.

Use a fabric pastry bag or parchment decorating cone, either one with its tip's opening cut to a three-fourths inch diameter to fill the mini-sculpture foundation. Parchment paper will suffice for a single figurine; however, a pastry bag can easily be refilled and is more expeditious when one is preparing more than one framework at a time.

Fill the foundations ahead of time to allow them to cure. Drying time of a day or more will help to set the icing and to prevent moisture from soaking into the absorbent ice cream cones. Decorating over uncured foundations can cause problems, as excessively moist ice cream cones may have a tendency to bend or to collapse.

Select only a type of buttercream that is firm and that tends to dry on the surface. The decorating buttercream formula at the beginning of Chapter I is recommended. Softer, creamy icings will impart too much moisture to the ice cream cone structure.

Cut each ice cream cone with sharp scissors or with a sharp knife. Make the cut quickly and accurately—speed will help to prevent the ice cream cone from shattering.

The mini-sculptures that follow are assembled in two basic sizes—Model "A" for figures with small heads, and Model "B" for figures with large heads.

CUT ICE CREAM CONES FOR THE FRAMEWORK

Model "A"—Prepare two cones.

First cone—Cut 1-7/8 inches from the pointed end of the cone. Retain the pointed end for the *head cone.*

Second cone—Cut 1-3/8 inches from the pointed end of the cone. Retain the large flared end of the cone for the *body cone.*

Set the *body cone* with its cut end up.

Insert the *head cone* "point" down, into the top of the *body cone.*

Model "B"—Prepare two cones.

First cone—Cut 3-1/4 inches from the pointed end of the cone. Retain the pointed end for the *head cone.*

Second cone—Cut 1-7/8 inches from the pointed end of the cone. Retain the large flared end of the cone for the *body cone.* (This pointed section could be reserved as an extra head for the Model "A" framework.)

Use that same assembly procedure which is suggested for Model "A."

ASSEMBLE THE ICE CREAM CONE FRAMEWORK

The procedures for assembling the frameworks are the same for either Model "A" or Model "B." After the *head cones* and *body cones* are fitted together, fill a pastry bag with buttercream. With the left hand (for right-handers), pick up the ice cream cone framework and hold the *head cone* firmly in position with the index finger. Insert the tip of the pastry bag as far as it will go into the inside of the *body cone* and apply pressure enough to fill the ice cream cone with buttercream as the tip of the pastry bag is withdrawn. Place the filled framework so that it is centered and bonded firmly onto a four-inch square of cardboard. Learn not to overfill the framework to such an extent that it will cause extra buttercream to squeeze out around the base of the *body cone.*

Insert a half length of plastic drinking straw downward through the *head cone* of the framework; continue to force it downward until it rests on the cardboard base. This straw will provide a sturdy reinforcement for the figure.

Complete the framework by using the pastry bag to fill the *head cone* with buttercream. After allowing this structure to cure, center it onto a decorating turntable—use a dab of icing as adhesive so that the ice cream cone cannot scoot around. It is now ready to receive the artistic finish.

PLACE THE MINI-SCULPTURE ON THE CAKE

Because of its height, a mini-sculpture is somewhat top heavy and should not be removed from its cardboard base. After deciding on its position, press the mini-sculpture's cardboard base firmly into the cake's icing. Cover the cardboard square with buttercream of any color by using a decorating cone that is fitted with a star tip. After the figure is in place, additional decorations are not necessary but they can be added to complement the mini-sculpture if extra flowers, etc., will help to create a better composition. This treatment is worthy of consideration particularly on large cakes, although the void can be filled with a fancy inner border if it is reasoned that additional decorations might detract from the figure.

The greeting can be piped with buttercream on the cake's surface or may be printed on an upright sign. A simple sign can be constructed with a square of white cardboard stapled to a plastic drinking straw. Print or write the message with a felt pen or with piping jell, but not with buttercream. Oils from the buttercream will soak into and will discolor the cardboard.

ANGEL

This mini-sculpture is formed over the Model "A" framework. The flesh color for the face and hands will require two parchment decorating cones; a large one with the opening in its tip cut to about the diameter of a milkshake straw, and a smaller one with its tip cut to a string-sized opening—for the facial details.

The angel's gown can be made in any desirable pastel tint. Whichever color the decorator selects should be placed in a large parchment cone that has been fitted with a Number 18 star tip.

The hair can be made with either a Number 16 or a Number 18 star tip. Other details of the head and face are left to the discretion of the decorator, since the faces for the angel, bride, or any other mini-doll can be as simple or as elaborate as the individual wishes.

PROCEDURE

Center the foundation on a turntable. Begin with the pastel gown. To pipe the head first would make it difficult to cover the *body cone,* since one might not be able to avoid damaging the face. The gown will cover the entire lower section from the cardboard base up to the neck (where the *head cone* and *body cone* are joined). Pipe tapered, vertical columns of buttercream with the star tip, around the circumference of the body. Begin each column with heavy pressure at the base, and relax the pressure gradually as the decorating cone is drawn upward. This will produce an even coverage of the flared ice cream cone.

Attend next to the head and the facial details. Use the large decorating cone of flesh-toned icing to cover the top and front of the *head cone.* Cover the top with a round swirl bubble, then use the same swirl method to build an oval face. Cover the sides of the *head cone* with flat columns of icing, but take into consideration the shapes of the profile and the jaw line. Add a thin coat of flesh color to cover any of the exposed neck area between the chin and the top of the gown.

Use a palette knife to shape the head into a form that resembles the basic buttercream head as was described in FIGURE PIPING AND THE HUMAN ANATOMY in the preceding chapter. Certain portions of the head may need an extra shot of buttercream here and there to accentuate some contours.

Smooth and sculpture the face, following the same steps that were observed in Chapter V. Complete the details of the face, then style the hair with graceful, flowing tresses.

Use the pastel buttercream to add arms—they should be bent so that the hands are raised in a prayerful pose. Add a ruffled collar of the same tone, or select a complementary contrast. Any additional lace or trim is optional.

Place a gold ring in her hair to represent a halo, and trace the accompanying drawing to create a pattern for the wings. The rounded side of a styrofoam cup will provide a perfect, non-absorbent material for the wings. Because the cup is curved, the second wing of each pair should be cut with the pattern flipped to the reverse side.

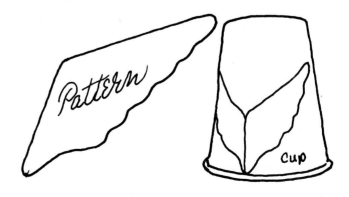

WITCH

Form the witch over a Model "A" foundation—its make-up is quite similar to that of the angel. Prepare three parchment decorating cones, one each of flesh color, grey, and black. Use sharp scissors to trim their tips to form openings equal to the diameter of a milkshake straw. Fill a smaller parchment cone with flesh-toned buttercream, and cut its point to a string-sized opening. Fit two parchment cones with Number 16 star tips, filling one with green and the other with straw-colored buttercream.

Cover the *body cone* with two rows of tapered vertical columns in place of the long, one-piece gown as was designed for the angel. Form the bottom row with grey icing. Pipe grey tapered columns from the base of the framework upward to about the middle of the *body cone*. Then, pipe black columns of buttercream so that they slightly overlap the top of the grey skirt, to form a cape around the upper half of the witch's body.

Make the old girl's face rather ugly with a pointed chin and a long nose. Her head can be piped very simply without a lot of attention given to smoothing the form. Green or yellow eyes with black centers will add to the eerie nature of this whimsical goblin (utilize the smaller decorating cones for the details).

284

With the cone of black icing, pipe an L-shaped sleeve on each side of the cape. Add a ruffled black collar and accents of black and grey to finish the cape and dress.

The cone of green buttercream will provide the wild, scraggly hairdo. Encircle the top of the head with a ring of black buttercream to form a brim, then pull a teardrop upward from the center of this ring to complete the pointed hat.

The broom handle is a wooden skewer, its point stuck into the cardboard base. Lean the skewer at an angle so that it crosses the body between the sleeves' ends. Pipe the witch's hands across the skewer to make it appear as though she is holding the broomstick. Use the straw-colored icing for the bristles on the end of the broom.

Place the mini-witch on a cake, cover the cardboard base of the sculpture with straw-colored grass, and add little orange pumpkins. Pipe other pumpkins and Jack O'Lanterns about the cake to carry out the Halloween theme. The greeting can be printed with wiggly lines to lend a scary touch. "Witching You a Happy Halloween" or "H-h-h-have a H-h-h-happy B-b-b-birthday!" will express the customer's wishes beautifully.

SANTA CLAUS

Use a preassembled Model "B" foundation for this jolly St. Nick. Center it on the turntable and ready three large parchment decorating cones. Fill one with flesh color, one with red, and the third with black. Cut each cone's tip to the diameter of a milkshake straw. Two more large cones fitted with Number 16 star tips should be filled: one with white buttercream, the other with bright green. Make up small parchment cones, fill one each with red, black, and white, then cut their tips to string-sized openings (for facial details and other trimmings).

The bell-shaped cup of the ice cream cone that was originally designed to hold a scoop of ice cream, will now become the foundation for Santa's stool. Just above the place where this bell begins to flare, there is usually a band that encircles the outside of the ice cream cone. Use this band as a guide to determine the height of the stool (to be formed after Santa's body is completed).

Start at the position for the top of the stool and apply red icing with the large decorating cone. Do this by turning the turntable while piping a thick band of buttercream that spirals, row-upon-row, upward to the top of the *body cone*. For a rounder body, repeat the process to add extra layers of icing. Smooth the body with the palette knife and the half-inch water color brush.

Cover the bell-shaped base of the ice cream cone to complete the stool. Use the decorating cone of green icing to apply the textured pattern with even, up-and-down strokes around the circumference of the armature.

Pipe the two red bubbles at the lower front side of the body for the legs. Then, use the large decorating cone of black buttercream to pipe boots down from the end of each knee, and also to encircle the center of his body with a black belt. Make use of the white buttercream in the star-tipped cone to add realistic, furry trim down his front and around the base of his coat.

Form two red, "L-" shaped sleeves and make flesh-colored bubbles for his hands. Complete the white fur trim over the ends of Santa's sleeves and the tops of his boots.

The simple face is an oval swirl bubble over the front of the *head cone*. Smooth the bubble with the palette knife and half-inch brush. Pipe the eyes and brows, then form the bubble-nose and the line for his mouth with the small parchment cone of red buttercream.

With the star-tipped decorating cone, cover the sides and back of his head with graceful waves of white hair and add a handsome moustache. The nightcap type hat is made with the large decorating cone of red icing, and is formed like a swirl bubble only with extra pressure at the finish to pull out a long point. Complete the pointed hat with a white furry tassle.

LEPRECHAUN

This little fellow can double either as a Christmas Elf or as a St. Patrick's Day Leprechaun. He is constructed like the Santa except for his brown beard and crossed legs. Each leg is piped over a bent short length of plastic bar straw that has been inserted into the *body cone* for support.

The log on which he rests is formed by two small pieces of cake, cut to proper size and shape. The texture of the dark brown bark is achieved with a star-tipped cone after the exposed ends of the log are covered with the circular pattern of light tan.

His clothing and hat can be green with yellow or red trim and his pointed shoes may be piped with buttercream in any contrasting color.

288

OWL

This wise old owl is constructed over a Model "B" armature. Prepare by mixing the proper colors and by filling the necessary parchment decorating cones. Use two large parchment cones—one of white, the other with medium grey buttercream—and cut the point of each cone with sharp scissors to form an opening equal in size to the diameter of a milkshake straw. Fit a third large parchment cone with a Number 16 star tip, and fill it with brown icing.

Make two smaller parchment cones, fill one with black, the other with yellow buttercream, and cut their tips to form string-sized openings. Fill one more small cone with orange buttercream and cut its tip to produce an opening comparable to the diameter of a milkshake straw.

Position the ice cream cone framework onto a turntable—apply a dab of icing for an adhesive. Use the large decorating cone of white icing for the owl's body—begin about half an inch above the flared bell at the base of the *body cone.* Start the column, and pipe it upward in a continuous swirl to the level of the owl's neck. Gradually build extra bulk at the middle of his body either by applying increased pressure, or by adding extra layers of the spiraling column. Use the same technique to build a nicely rounded head; however, the spiral of buttercream also should continue upward to cover the top of the *head cone.*

Employ the star-tipped cone of brown buttercream to cover the bell of the *body cone* with vertical, textured columns to resemble the bark on a stump, to create a perch for Mr. Wisebird.

289

The feathers for the tummy and the rest of the owl's body also are made with the large decorating cones. Each feather is an individually piped teardrop, formed vertically with a short, upward stroke. Begin by forming a single row of teardrops across the base of the body. Then add the next row of feathers so that it slightly overlaps the previous row, "shingle" fashion, the feathering process is complete.

The owl's tummy must be covered with white feathers. Remember to start at the bottom and to cover only the front of the body with a row just wide enough to form a nice, fat tummy. Use the same decorating cone to produce a "C"-shaped foundation at either side of the face to support the spiraled discs on the front of the head. Make flat swirl bubbles for the two discs that shape the face.

Now turn the owl around so that it faces the back of the turntable. With the bird in this position, pipe teardrop formations in a fan-shaped pattern to form the owl's tail. Use the large decorating cone of grey buttercream for his tail and for the remaining body feathers.

Pipe the bottom row of grey feathers, beginning at one side of the white tummy. Form one teardrop beside the other around the back of the body until the row is completed where it meets the other edge of the tummy section. Add shingled layers of feathers, upward over the contours of the body, then over the back and sides of the head. Face the bird forward and finish the top of the head by aiming the pointed ends of the last rows of feathers toward the center of the face in a fan formation.

Outline the two white discs with a thin ruffle of grey buttercream, using very light pressure. The ear-like feathery horns at each side of the top of its head are simple teardrops pulled to a point with the grey buttercream. Pipe two slim lines in a "V," beginning each side at the center of the face, and relaxing the pressure so that each line becomes a part of the point where it meets the feathered "ear."

Add two wings, following the example illustrated in the photograph. Use teardrop feathers and try to keep the directions of their lines like those in the illustration so as to form each wing as realistically as possible.

Pipe two black circles for the outlines of the eyes. Fill in these outlines with the small decorating cone of yellow buttercream. Complete each eye with a black bubble for a pupil and add small black speckles on the owl's breast.

Finish this handsome bird with the small cone of orange buttercream by pulling teardrop formations out and downward to form his gracefully arched beak and claws.

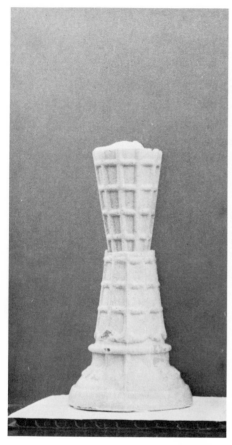

TEDDY BEAR

Use a Model "B" armature to support this replica of a cuddly Teddy Bear. Prepare a large parchment of cinnamon-brown buttercream for the main portions of the head and body. Cut the tip of this cone to form an opening about 3/8 of an inch in diameter. Fit another large decorating cone with a Number 16 star tip and fill the cone with grassy-green buttercream to cover the pedestal on which the bear is seated.

Make up four smaller parchment cones; the first to be filled with black buttercream, the second with white. Cut the tips of each of these cones to form string-sized openings. Fill the remaining parchment cones—one with red, the other with honey-colored icing—and cut their tips to the diameter of a milkshake straw.

Pipe cinnamon-brown icing in a spiral over the entire body, from the neck down to the place where the rim of his stool will begin. Smooth the body with a palette knife and one of the widest brushes. Build a spiral of buttercream to shape the head into a nice full ball; then, gently smooth the formation.

Cover the flared base of the *body cone* with green buttercream, employing up-and-down strokes, in the manner as was described in the formation of Santa's stool.

Pipe the bear's fore and hind legs with brown buttercream to match the rest of his body. Add two bubbles at either side of his head to make the foundations for the ears. Make a large bubble of honey-colored buttercream for the bear's muzzle, and use the same decorating cone to over-pipe the edge of each ear-foundation so as to create a natural looking outer rim around the ear.

Follow the illustrations to complete the facial details, using the small decorating cones of the black and the white buttercream. The bow tie is piped with red icing.

Pastel colors can be substituted for the more natural brown tones if the decorator or customer prefers. Yellow or pink bears make delightful baby shower decorations. See the photographs for the example of another alternative—the handsome little "panda."

When using this mini-sculpture on a cake, add colorful daisies or other suitable flowers. Use a catch greeting like: "I Couldn't BEAR to Miss Your Birthday!" Pipe little honey bees around the flowers and add a miniature beehive with "I Love You, HONEY," or "BEE Happy, It's Your Birthday!"

293

SCULPTURED CAKES

Working with cake as a sculptor's material requires careful planning. The engineering concerns of "stress" and "support" are the greatest problems to be encountered. Each figure must have an armature (the framework or supporting structure within a sculpture). This framework can be designed only after the artist draws, to scale, front and side views of the figure according to the way the finished sculpture should appear.

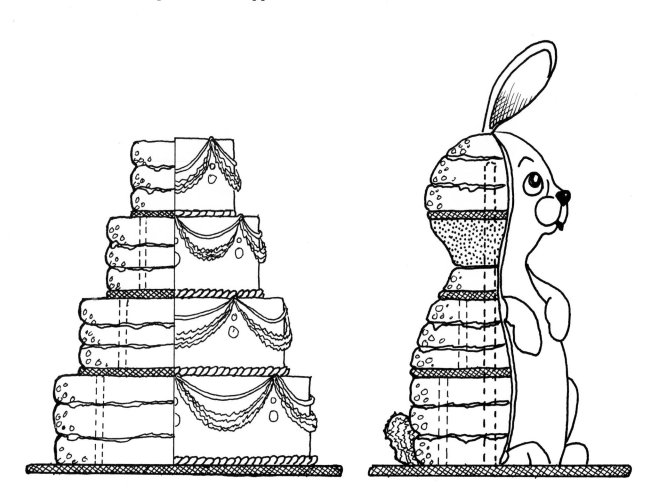

FRAMEWORK

The armature for a sculptured cake is patterned after the supporting structure of a stacked wedding cake. For instance, the foundation for a stacked round wedding cake requires a large, primary platform and a series of pre-cut discs (subordinate platforms), supported usually by wooden or plastic dowels. The size of each disc is comparable to the diameter of that tier which it bears. Whereas the dimensions of these discs are easy to establish once the decorator knows the given size of the wedding cake, the subordinate platforms of an armature for a sculptured cake are difficult to determine. Each must be cut according to the shape of the cross-section of the figures at each different level where the sculpture is to be supported. These levels will occur at the top of about every three layers of cake.

Either "pound" or "sponge" cake seems to work better for sculpturing than does any other of the many varieties. These types of cakes are less tender and provide strength with a minimum amount of shrinkage. For most figures, the cakes should be baked in sheet pans, so as to permit the artist to cut layers of any shape and size that the job may require. The height of three layers of this cake, when they are filled and stacked, should measure about four inches (thickness will vary with each type of cake, so measure accordingly). This measurement, less about 3/16 inch which one should allow for shrinkage, will provide the proper spacing for the subordinate platforms on the armature.

Use this measurement on the scale drawing of the figure to mark the positions for each subordinate platform. From this drawing, the artist must estimate the approximate size and shape of the top of each section of the figure; then, he must cut cardboard patterns of those shapes to use as guides for cutting layers from the sheet cakes. To do this, one has to visualize accurately how each section would look if the sculpture were sliced in two at the level for one of the subordinate platforms, and were viewed from overhead.

Each sculpture, like a wedding cake, must also have a primary platform for the base. This is usually a piece of one-half inch (or thicker) plywood, with its width equal to at least two-thirds the height of the sculpture. This width is absolutely necessary to prevent the sculpture from tipping over during transit.

For almost any tall, narrow sculpture, a single wooden or metal rod will have to extend through the center of the figure from the primary platform nearly to the top of its head. This rod acts as a "backbone" for the figure. In such cases, the subordinate platforms must have holes drilled to allow them to be slid down over the center rod. In addition to the center rod, each subordinate platform must be supported by pins (plastic straws or wooden dowels) through the lower mass of cake.

Sometimes it is necessary to have a secondary platform. When the base of a sculpture is supported on legs, the secondary platform will sit atop them and must be fastened firmly to those legs with screws or rivets. If the figure is tall and narrow, like that of the human body, the center rod still must be used, but it will fasten to the secondary platform.

Four-legged animals, when standing on all fours, do not require the center rod on the secondary platform as their bodies are not very deep by comparison to their width. In its place, an upright piece of plywood, cut to the shape of the animal's neck, will support a platform for its head.

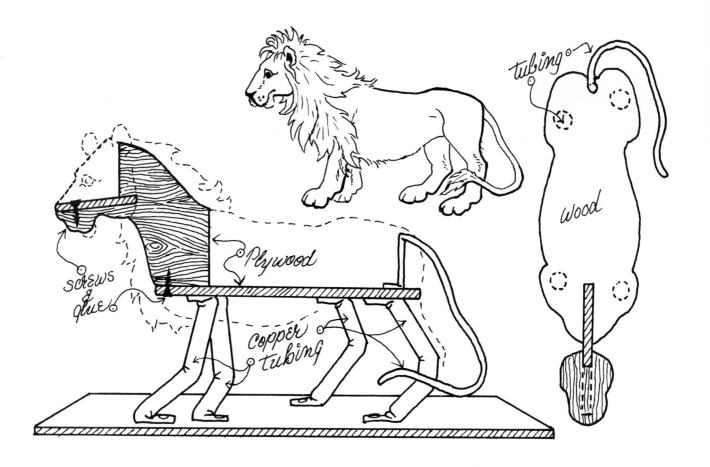

The reinforcements for the legs of smaller animal sculptures can be made from copper tubing, bent to the proper angles. Firm pieces of cardboard, cut in the silhouetted shape of each leg and fastened to the outer side of each of the copper tube legs, will provide the appropriate contours and will act as a foundation for the buttercream covering. For larger animals, supports in the shape of legs can be cut from plywood. To add thickness to the upper portion of these wooden legs, it may be necessary to shape "plastic foam" pads and to glue them into position.

The legs (if the sculpture requires them), and some of the other parts of the armature should be cut and preassembled before the artist begins to cut the cake. With the scale drawing as a guide, the decorator must cut plywood for the primary platform (also the secondary platform, if one is to be used) and for the one subordinate platform that will support the head.

All masses must be supported. For instance, if the sculptured figure is to have an extended arm, the extended portion of that arm must be made over some form of foundation. In such a case, the extended foundation should be fastened to, or be designed as part of, one of the subordinate platforms of the armature.

If the sculpture is to be a creature on four legs, the artist will need also to cut an upright support in the shape of the animal's neck (include enough material to extend down through its shoulders so that it can be fastened to the secondary platform). The upper, front edge of the neck piece should be designed with a spur which is shaped like the lower jaw of the animal. This spur will support the subordinate platform which will bear the bulk of the animal's head.

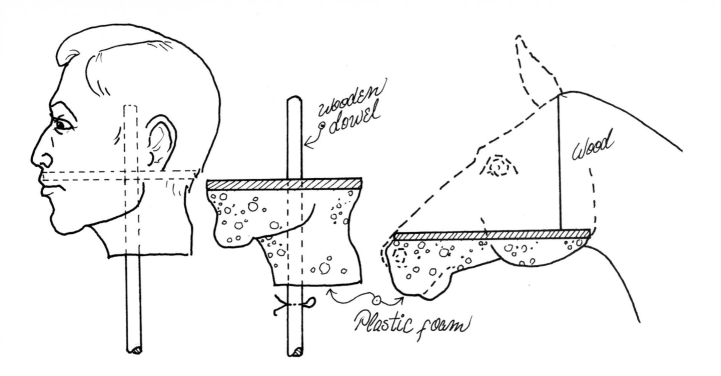

The platform for the head of either an animal or a human should be patterned from a cross-section of the scale drawing, at a line that bisects the skull from the mouth line (upper lip) through the lower back of the jaw. The other subordinate platforms for the sculpture can be cut after the cake has been shaped, prior to its final assembly with buttercream filling. This procedure will be explained in greater detail with the accompanying illustrations that follow.

Any part of a sculpture which is suspended below one of the platforms, and which is smaller than that platform, must be made from plastic foam. This will include the mass beneath the "head platform," which forms the lower part of the jaws and the neck, and also the belly portion that is suspended below the secondary platform of an animal sculpture. The upright neck support for four-legged animals can be padded on both sides, either with plastic foam (for larger sculptures) or with layers of cake.

The plastic foam pads and body formations can easily be shaped with a knife or a hacksaw blade. A serrated knife blade works almost like a saw on the plastic foam for roughing out the shape, and final smoothing can be achieved with coarse sandpaper.

When the plastic forms are ready for assembling, they can be glued securely to the plywood components. Many glues cause plastic to disintegrate, so be sure to use a type of non-toxic adhesive that is waterproof and will not harm plastics. Some of the powdered glues designed for laminating wood are good, and one needs only to mix the amount required for a particular job. It's a good idea to allow several hours for the glued pieces to dry before assembling the armature.

All the pieces of the armature that are connected to the primary or secondary platforms should be fastened as securely as possible with glue and screws, rivets or heavy-duty staples. Always take special precautions to prevent stray hardware and plastic foam particles from finding their way into cake scraps. Throughly clean the work area, before working with the cake, to avoid any contamination from such foreign matter.

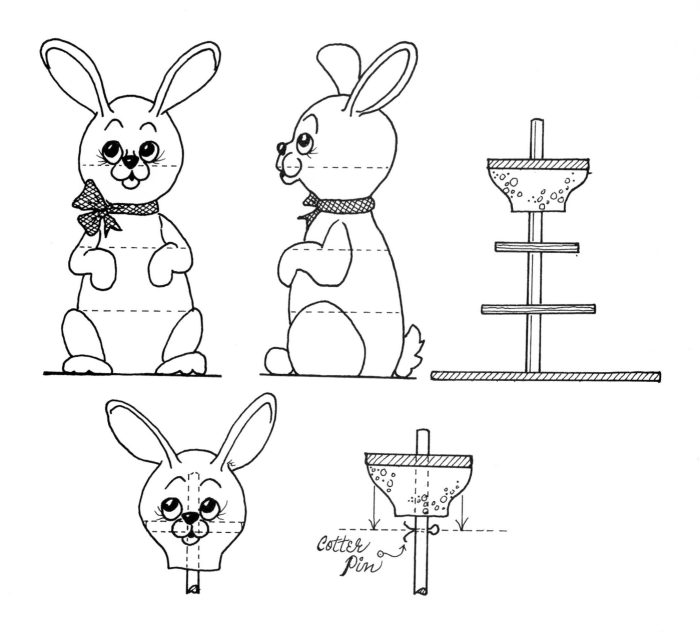

Sketch two views (front and side) of the figure as it should appear after it is sculptured. Small figures, under twenty-four inches in height, should be drawn to actual size. Larger sculptures may be drawn to scale, but the dimensions should be exact. Draw lines across the figures to designate those positions for the subordinate platforms.

Cut and assemble the basic components of the armature. Make certain, if the armature has a center rod, that the head platform will slide over the shaft. It should fit snugly without binding. Hold the platform in its proper position on the rod and draw a mark on the rod at the base of the plastic foam neck. A small hole, drilled through the rod at this mark, will accommodate a cotter pin to support the weight of the sculptured head.

298

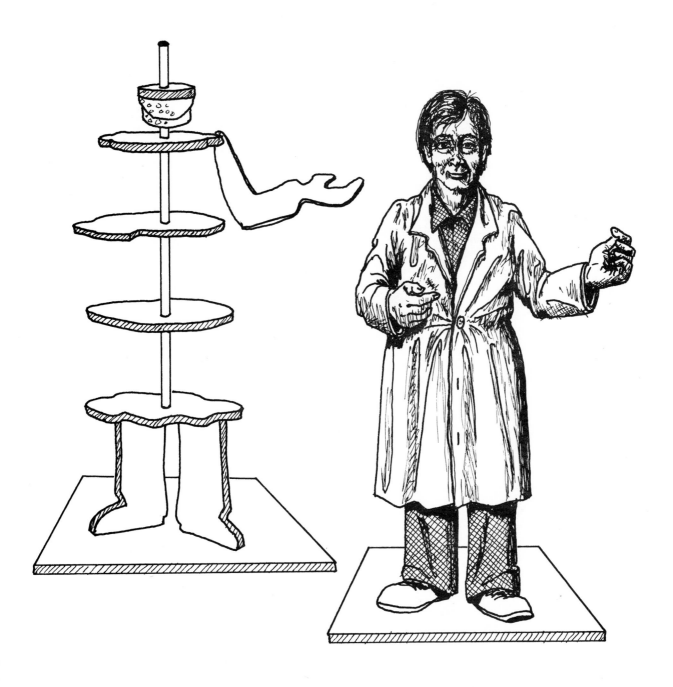

Each sculpture will require its own individual framework, designed specifically for that purpose. This requires careful study of the preliminary drawings and analysis of the points of stress. This will amount to some trial and error methods for the beginner, but careful planning will many times prevent early misjudgments. A student needs not to be discouraged by a failure if he uses it as a lesson to avoid similar mistakes in the future.

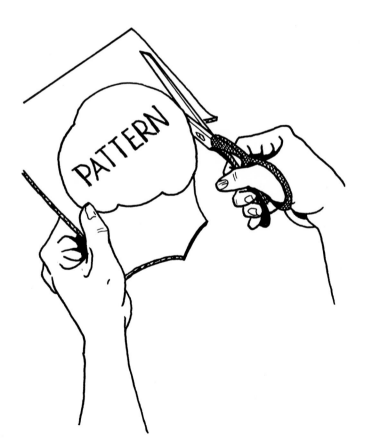

SHAPE LAYERS FROM SHEET CAKES

Draw and cut cardboard patterns, one for each cross-section indicated by the lines that were marked on the drawings to designate the positions of the subordinate platforms. Use these patterns as guides to cut the necessary layers from sheet cakes. When cutting each layer, take into consideration any part of that section of the sculpture where the figure changes shape, and be sure to cut the layer large enough to allow for that change.

Cut a hole in the center of each layer, just large enough to allow the cake to be slid down over the armature's rod. Stack all the layers, without filling, together in their proper order, comparing the rough structure with the drawings. Carefully sculpture the cake to a more exact shape, eliminating any excessive bulk, and defining the basic features. Make certain that each portion of the form coincides with the shape and position of its equal in the drawing. Disassemble the layers, carefully noting their order so that they can be replaced in their original positions.

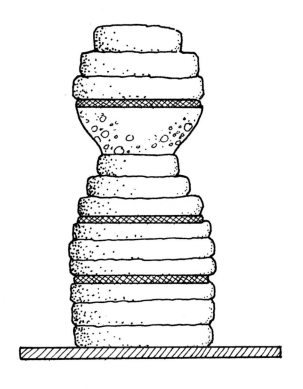

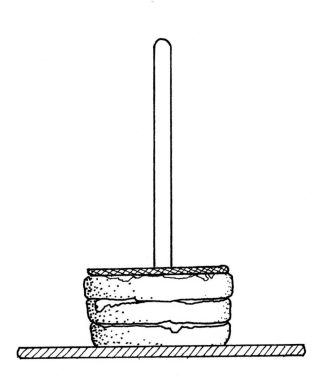

Fill and stack the three bottom layers and place them onto the armature. Cut and insert straws or dowels into these layers, then ice the top. Use the shape of the next layer in line to trace a pattern for that subordinate platform which will occupy this position. Cut the platform slightly smaller than the pattern so that none of it will accidentally show through the finished sculpture. This platform may be made from corrugated cardboard (use plywood for large, heavy figures). By cutting the subordinate platform smaller than the cake layer, one allows for any cake shrinkage that may occur and also the artist is permitted to do any last-minute trimming that may be necessary.

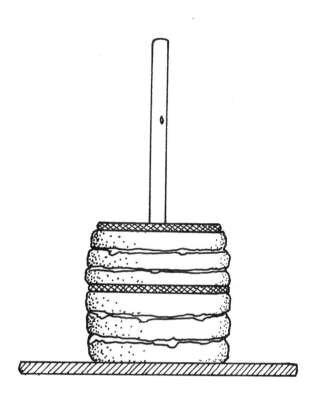

Slip the subordinate platform over the center rod and press it firmly onto the first stack of cake. Ice the top of the platform and proceed by assembling each three-layered section, in the same manner, to complete each major segment of the figure. Usually a figure will have two major segments, the body and the head. The body sits on either the primary or the secondary platform. Remember that the head rests on its own plywood platform, cut to the shape of a cross-section of the skull. Quarter-inch plywood is fine for heads up to about four inches in diameter.

When the cake is stacked onto the framework, try to visualize how it will appear when the details are completed in icing. If any portions of the cake need to be reshaped, or if the skull needs more hollowing for the eye sockets or the temples, or if the mouth area needs to be narrowed, this is the time to do it. Brush and blow away all excess crumbs. An airbrush works well for this, but don't hold its nozzle so close to the cake that the air pressure blasts holes in the cake's surface.

ENROBE THE CAKE WITH BUTTERCREAM

When icing a sculpture of a seated or erect-standing figure, begin with the head. If the subject is an animal on all fours, start at the top of its back. Apply the icing, using a cone with its tip cut large enough to allow the most desirable thickness of icing for the job; or use the Number 180 rose tip, reshaped for edging a sheet cake, to apply the covering over large, flat surfaces (see the listing: ALL PURPOSE EDGING TIP in CHAPTER I). Be sure to select the proper color of icing for each specific part of the figure. Preliminary smoothing and shaping of the form is done with the palette knife and final detail is achieved with the half-inch or one-inch water color brush, just as it was explained in the method for smoothing piped figures.

Ruffled or very coarse hair and fur may require the use of a star tip. In such a case, start layering the fur from the base of the figure, adding each row in shingle fashion so that it overlaps the one before. For a sleeker coat of fur, cover the figure by following the same technique as was suggested on the previous page, smooth it with a palette knife, but instead of using the water color brushes, comb in the texture with a coarse-bristled paint brush. A common house painting brush works very effectively for this kind of texturing, but it should be dampened frequently and then wiped clean after each stroke.

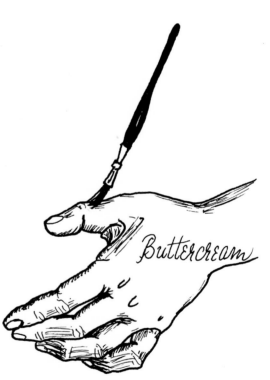

Ears and delicate fingers can be formed over carefully shaped pieces of cardboard that are inserted in the proper positions. Once they are in place, pipe the icing formations directly onto the cardboard pieces and shape them with the palette knife and brushes.

HUMPTY DUMPTY SCULPTURE

A simple figure which will afford valuable experience in sculpturing, and will demonstrate the value of the Number 180 edging tip, and one which can be easily introduced into production, is this attractive Humpty Dumpty Cake.

Prepare a doubled quarter-sheet board (9″ x 13″) for the primary platform—two boards glued together to provide adequate support. Use a seven-inch cardboard cake round under the body while the cake is being shaped and iced.

A center rod will not be necessary for the construction of this figure. Most any standard cake will work; however, chocolate is somewhat more difficult to cover.

The egg-shaped body for Humpty Dumpty will require four eight-inch layers and one six-inch layer arranged so that the smaller layer is centered on top. Stack the layers, without filling, on the seven-inch cake circle and place the assembled cake on a turntable. Turn the cake while shaping its sides with a sharp knife. Hold the knife at a steady angle to carve away rings of cake, varying the angle of the cut for each ring. Shape the upper half of the form to resemble the smooth, small end of an egg. This shaping should be limited to that portion of cake which is above the middle of the third layer, so that the full diameter of the center layers is maintained in Humpty's mid-section. The bottom layer should be beveled slightly inward at the base to suggest a more nearly oval body. Round the sides of the oval as smoothly as possible.

Disassemble the layers and replace the lower three, this time, with filling to bond them together. Cut plastic straw supports and insert them. Ice the top of the third layer and cut a platform circle of corrugated cardboard, just smaller than the bottom of the fourth layer of cake. Secure the platform to the first three layers and cover the cardboard with icing. Press the remaining filled layers in proper sequence atop the platform to complete the structure.

Use the Number 180 edging tip to completely cover the form with white icing, while rotating the cake on a turntable so as to allow a smooth and even application. Smooth away as many ridges as possible with a limber bowl knife or palette knife and finish the surface with the one-inch brush and hot water. Use only sufficient water to do the job and try to avoid leaving the surface dripping wet. If the surface becomes excessively damp, allow the cake to dry before attempting to finish the sculpture.

The clothing should be done in any desirable bright color, with the top of the collar about two and one-half inches above the base of the cake. Pipe Humpty's one-piece suit of clothes with a Number 125 rose tip, but first use a small cone that is filled with icing of that same color to mark a guide line for the height of his collar.

Before removing the cake from the turntable, pipe on the facial features. The nose can be a red gum ball, hollowed with a skewer and placed over a half-length of plastic bar straw that is inserted into the cake. If a gum ball is not available, pipe a bubble of red buttercream, but make certain that it is fastened securely.

The mouth, eyes and brows are piped with black buttercream. Use a small parchment decorating cone with its tip cut to a string-sized opening.

Leave the cake on the seven-inch round and secure the round to the board with glue. Situate the cake enough toward one end of the quarter-sheet board so as to allow sufficient room for the legs and feet. Prepare two ice cream cones by cutting off the bell-shaped ends, then snip just enough off their pointed ends to allow for passage of plastic straws.

Cover the ice cream cones with the same color buttercream that was used for the suit. Place the two iced cones at the front base of the body so that they angle, pointed ends outward. Then cut cardboard shoe soles like the pattern and staple them to the ends of drinking straws. Cover the cardboard shoes by rubbing black icing over them with the fingers. Insert the straws through the ice cream cone legs and into the cake.

Use milkshake straws, bent to the proper angles, and position them as foundations for the arms. Overpipe them with icing to match the color of the rest of the clothing and add white icing gloves to finish the uniform. Add a belt and bow tie with a plain cone of any color that will contrast with the suit.

The five-inch diameter brim of the hat is cut from cardboard with a three-inch circle removed from the center so that it is shaped like a ring. Rub straw-colored icing over the entire surface of the brim and situate it on top of the cake. A three-inch circle of cake, centered over the top of the ring and secured with a short length of plastic drinking straw serves as a crown for the hat. Finish the hat with the straw-colored icing in a small parchment cone fitted with a Number 16 star tip.

Voila, Mr. Humpty Dumpty! This little guy will cheer the heart of many a delighted youngster. Such a cake with a fracture line and a bandage piped on to replace the hat, would make a cheery "Get Well" cake for a person convalescing from a fall. Or, a regular Humpty Dumpty could be suggested for a boss or friend if Mr. Dumpty's hands were clasped around the sign reading, "Happy Birthday to a 'Good Egg'."

Pattern

Happy Birthday

Powell

311

EPILOGUE

Cake art cannot be separated from "art," the general term. Cake decorating, however, attempted without the knowledge of color and composition, and applied without an understanding of proportion and balance, can only loosely be classified as art. Art is not an accident. It is more than just a faithful reproduction of objects or of people around us—*art is communication.* Through palette, sculpture, mime and dance, and yes, even cake art, the artist is communicating —not verbally, but visually. He is creating the first stage of a dialogue—a transmission of feelings to touch the emotions of the observer. The observer, if the work is truly a thing of art, will respond emotionally, completing the dialogue. A message will have indeed been exchanged, just as surely as if words had been spoken. This places a great responsibility upon the artist. To fulfill this role in the visual arts, one must be cognizant of every detail concerning his subject. He must be keenly aware of everything around him. By observing, really observing, he can learn to see those things so obscure that they are completely overlooked by the average person. Herein lies the artist's greatest contribution to mankind. Through one man's talents and through his sensitivity to the abstract details of the world about him, he is able to share a bit of beauty which may otherwise have gone undetected in life's hurried pace.

Sensitive observation and knowledge of the theories of art (color, composition, proportion, and balance) are as important to the cake decorator as they are to any other artist. Even in production decorating, one should use these important elements. Yes, training takes time! To acquire any knowledge and to learn how to use it takes time; but once accomplished, it will take a highly skilled decorator no longer to create a design with eye-pleasing color combinations and good composition, than that time which it would require for a poorly trained decorator to complete an awkwardly planned decoration.

To be an artist does take a certain aptitude, but the inborn talent is not the total answer. Knowing the right method, and knowing how to avoid doing something in the wrong way, is more important. With the proper artistic training, anyone can do a better than average job.

This training coupled with artistic talent and matched with imagination is a combination found in the great decorators of today. Mix these components with a curiosity to seek new and original forms of decorating, and therein will lie tomorrow's new realms of cake art.